"This deeply grounded, ethnographic account of border crossings is exactly the sort of book we nee the dynamics of human smuggling and to demystii petuated by politicians and the media. Anyone ii gling actually works, especially works, especially along the Arizona–Mexico border, should read this book."

Peter Andreas, John Hay Professor of Political Science and International Studies, Brown University, USA

"There has been much media coverage of irregular border crossings between the US and its southern neighbor, but few have engaged in a careful and systematic examination of the topic like the one presented here by Dr. Gabriella Sanchez. Through extensive court record reviews, in-depth interviews with both human smugglers and undocumented migrants, and extended field observations, Dr. Sanchez unpacks the complex and often mutually-enabling dynamics between those who wish to cross illegally into the US and those who are ready to facilitate for a fee. Dr. Sanchez's nuanced analysis of the political tensions in immigration control, informal economy along border communities, and gendered work in the smuggling enterprise has set a new standard for others to follow and emulate."

Sheldon Zhang, Professor, Department of Sociology, San Diego State University, USA

"Human Smuggling and Border Crossings is a landmark book on an epochal issue for Arizona, the United States, and the twenty-first century world. At the same time deeply personal and coolly objective, the book provides a unique insight into the lived experiences of smuggling, for migrants, smugglers, and the authorities, and in so doing explodes many of the myths that have distorted our understanding and policy responses to human smuggling."

Khalid Koser, Deputy Director, Geneva Centre for Security Policy, Switzerland

"The motives of migrants are well known to scholars and students, but studies about the lives of those they trust to guide them are often confused by theory, rhetoric and fear. With a clear, even literary hand, Dr. Sanchez guides us through the struggles and structures of non-violent smugglers, narrating their realities and explaining their experiences. I have yet to read a more thorough, insightful or empathetic account of the oft-maligned, yet little understood people who cross both real and imaginary borders to move others from anarchy to safety."

David J. Danelo, Director of Field Research, Foreign Policy Research Institute, USA

Human Smuggling and Border Crossings

Graphic narratives of tragedies involving the journeys of irregular migrants trying to reach destinations in the global north are common in the media and are blamed almost invariably on human smuggling facilitators, described as rapacious members of highly structured underground transnational criminal organizations, who take advantage of migrants and prey upon their vulnerability.

This book contributes to the current scholarship on migration by providing a window into the lives and experiences of those behind the facilitation of irregular border crossing journeys. Based on fieldwork conducted among coyotes in Arizona—the main point of entry for irregular migrants into the United States at the turn of the twenty-first century—this project goes beyond traditional narratives of victimization and financial exploitation and asks: who are the men and women behind the journeys of irregular migrants worldwide? How and why do they enter the human smuggling market? How are they organized? How do they understand their roles in transnational migration? How do they explain the violence and victimization so many migrants face while in transit?

This book is suitable for students and academics involved in the study of migration, border enforcement, and migrant and refugee criminalization.

Gabriella E. Sanchez is an anthropologist by training and a graduate of Arizona State University's Justice and Social Inquiry Program. Her research interests include borders, migration and transnational crime and labor. She has conducted fieldwork along the US–Mexico border, Mexico, Central America, North Africa, the Middle East and Australia, documenting the experiences of the men and women involved in drug and human smuggling operations as traffickers/smugglers. A Boren and a Fulbright fellow, Gabriella was also a post-doctoral researcher at the University of Maryland's Consortium for the Study of Terrorism and Responses to Terrorism (START) and a visiting lecturer on Feminism and Transnational Migration at Wellesley College. Gabriella is currently Assistant Professor at The Catholic University of America in Washington, DC and a Research Fellow at Monash University in Melbourne, Australia.

Routledge Studies in Criminal Justice, Borders and Citizenship
Edited by
Katja Franko Aas, University of Oslo
Mary Bosworth, University of Oxford
Sharon Pickering, Monash University

Globalizing forces have had a profound impact on the nature of contemporary criminal justice and law more generally. This is evident in the increasing salience of borders and mobility in the production of illegality and social exclusion. *Routledge Studies in Criminal Justice, Borders and Citizenship* showcases contemporary studies that connect criminological scholarship to migration studies and explore the intellectual resonances between the two. It provides an opportunity to reflect on the theoretical and methodological challenges posed by mass mobility and its control. By doing that, it charts an intellectual space and establishes a theoretical tradition within criminology to house scholars of immigration control, race, and citizenship including those who traditionally publish *either* in general criminological *or* in anthropological, sociological, refugee studies, human rights and other publications.

Human Smuggling and Border Crossings

Gabriella E. Sanchez

Routledge
Taylor & Francis Group

LONDON AND NEW YORK

First published 2015
by Routledge
2 Park Square, Milton Park, Abingdon, Oxfordshire OX14 4RN

and by Routledge
711 Third Avenue, New York, NY 10017

First issued in paperback 2016

Routledge is an imprint of the Taylor & Francis Group, an informa business

British Library Cataloguing in Publication Data
A catalogue record for this book is available from the British Library

Library of Congress Cataloging-in-Publication Data
Sanchez, Gabriella E.
Human smuggling and border crossings/Gabriella E. Sanchez.
Pages cm.—(Routledge studies in criminal justice, borders and citizenship)
1. Human smuggling. 2. Transnational crime. I. Title.
JV6201.S26 2014
364.1'37—dc23
2014019033

ISBN13: 978-1-138-23087-3 (pbk)
ISBN13: 978-0-415-70361-1 (hbk)

Typeset in Times New Roman
by Swales & Willis Ltd, Exeter, Devon, UK

To David and Flor, who taught me to cross borders.

Contents

Illustrations

Map

Table

Acknowledgements

When J. R. R. Tolkien said that not all those who wander are lost, he did not have me in mind. After years of wandering along borders, I was fortunate to find a destination in Monash University, where Sharon Pickering and her team at the Border Crossing Observatory gave me an academic home. Rebecca Powell, Julie Ham and Brandy Cochrane fueled my veins with Melbourne's fantastic coffee. Paddy Rawlinson, Anne McNevin, Marie Segrave, Mary Bosworth and Jude McCulloch consistently encouraged my work and provided infinite support.

Neither my search nor the wandering started in Australia, however. The quest into the social dynamics of human smuggling started many years back, working the detention area of Maricopa County Superior Court in Arizona alongside Chauncey Crenshaw and Tanya Kluender. It took shape at the School of Justice and Social Inquiry at Arizona State University among Nancy Jurik, Marjorie Zatz, Marie Provine, Mary Margaret Fonow, Mary Romero, Gaku Tsuda and Nancy Winn. It was also nourished and cultivated through my friendships with Carin Koenig, Cesar Cordova and Nayeli Burgueño, the love and the patience of Richard Martinez, Rita Urquijo-Ruiz, Eduardo Sanchez and Ana Evangelista, the mentorship of Sheldon Zhang and Arturo Aldama and Apollonia's companionship.

I attribute the ever present wanderlust, however, to my grandparents, David Evangelista and Florentina Benitez, and to my uncle, Gene Evangelista, who invited me to join them in their journeys—both the real and the imaginary ones—across valleys, rivers and mountains; who took me on their crusades through the recondite towns of Michoacán and the mythical neighborhoods of Mexico City. It was they who instilled in me the hunger for distant lands and faces, and who taught me of the inherent dignity of all forms of labor, of their redeeming power.

This same hunger took me to not so faraway places where I met others who have shown me new paths: Rens Lee and John Lyle in DC; Lupe, Alfredo, Adi and Kim Benitez in Chicago; Julia Carrillo-Lerma in Paris; and Lilly, Agustin, Cinthia, Leslie, Paola, David and Maria in Salt Lake City. It also took me to Wellesley College, where Rosanna Hertz, Chair of Women's and Gender Studies, alongside the students in my Transnational Migration and Gender Seminar—Mari Oceja, Shelby Baptista, Asia Sims, Lauren Walsh, Ferni Cruz and Quinn Willer—helped me survive Boston's inclement weather, and to East Los Angeles, to the home of my *comadre* Llesenia Trujillo and her family, whose friendship brought back into my life the happiness I had thought long lost. It eventually brought me back to the US Southwest, to the hallways of the University of Arizona, where Professors Raquel Rubio-Goldsmith and Anna O'Leary gave me the last push of *valentía* that I needed.

Julia Farrell worked incessantly on my manuscript during my erratic itineraries across four continents, providing invaluable copy-editing assistance. To her I am especially grateful. Heidi Lee at Routledge kept me sane in front of looming deadlines that seemed insurmountable. Thanks go to The Border Film Project, who selflessly shared the cover photograph from its collection, and to Yuri Herrera, whose words in the voice of Makina accompanied me along borders and preface Chapters 1, 4 and 5 of this book.

My life, however, would never have been what it is today without those who over the years have shared with me their stories—those who have allowed me to join them on their journeys, who have selflessly provided me with the testimonies you are about to read. While this book is an academic endeavor, it also sought to be a reflection of border crossers' voices—and their sense of loss and despair, but also of their hopes, courage and joy. This book is therefore dedicated to those who cross borders, and to those who assist them in their crossings with dignity and pride, caring for their needs and their safety. It is also for those who never completed the journey, but who dreamed of the day they would. This book is for those who cross rivers, deserts, oceans and foreign lands—from Juarez to Ceuta to the Sinai; from Tijuana to Istanbul to Al Taqaddum—looking for a safe area to resupply, for a place of respite away from the frontlines. This book is for them.

Abbreviations

IRCA	*Immigration Reform and Control Act*
MCAO	Maricopa County Attorney's Office
MCSO	Maricopa County Sheriff's Office
NGO	Non-governmental organization
PCOMO	Pima County Office of the Medical Examiner
SWAT	Special Weapons and Tactics Operations Team
US	United States

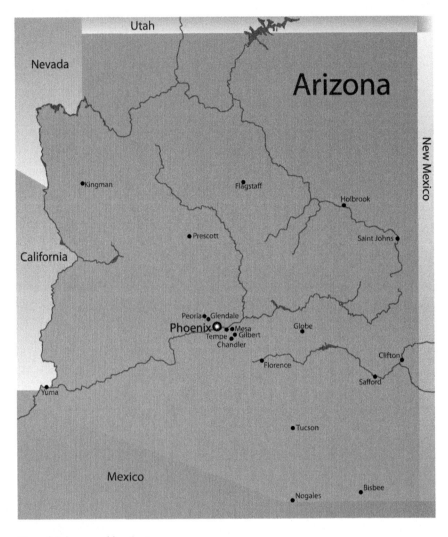

Map of Arizona and border towns

Source: Image courtesy of Shutterstock

Introduction
Among coyotes

You will cross, said Mr Q. He was not asking. You will cross, repeated Mr Q and now it sounded like an order. You will cross and get wet and will deal with sons of bitches; you will go desperate, of course, you will marvel and eventually you will find your brother and even if you are sad you will arrive wherever you have to arrive. Once there, there will be people who will take care of your needs.

He said it all with great clarity, without much emphasis, without moving a muscle. Suddenly, he stopped talking, grabbed Makina's hand in his and said "this is your heart—can you see it?"

(Yuri Herrera 2010, *Señales que precederán al fin del mundo* *[Signs that will precede the end of the world]*)

In the fall of 2000, after a brief and painful stint as a clerk in the Family Court—the section in charge of divorces and child custody battles—I begged a human resources employee at the Maricopa County Superior Court in Arizona for a transfer. I had been hoping for a chance to move to a department in which I did not have to deal with the anger of couples, the fears of children or the shouting matches of attorneys. Without showing much interest in my concerns, she told me about an opening in Criminal Court where, she said, I would "do interviews." She asked if I had any prior experience with interviewing, and fearing that if I said otherwise I would be sent back to the divorce window, I lied and said I did. She also wanted to know if I spoke Spanish and if I didn't mind driving to distant sections of the county. "Anything," I said, "I will do anything to leave Family Court."

Little did I know that I would spend most of the following seven years conducting interviews for presentence reports. Presentence reports are court-ordered documents that provide a summary of the legal facts involving a criminal offense from the perspective of all the parties involved and that provide sentencing recommendations to the judge presiding over the case. Among other documentation like victim statements, police accounts, court motions and background checks, the reports require the completion of a face-to-face meeting with the accused party—which constitutes the actual presentence interview. Many of the accused are in custody at local detention centers waiting for the conclusion of their cases at the time the interview is ordered.

Every week I would drive to the four detention centers in Maricopa County to complete these interviews. Given my language skills, most cases I was assigned involved Spanish-speaking detainees, the majority of whom were undocumented Mexican migrants. For most of my interviewees, our encounter was the first opportunity they had to discuss their case with someone fluent in Spanish without the need of an interpreter, which frequently facilitated our communication and my ability to develop rapport. Given the ethnicity of my clients and my own, as well as the nature of the cases that I was consistently assigned (drug trafficking, human smuggling, intoxicated driving and domestic violence charges), it was not long before I became interested in the interplay of race in the context of the American criminal justice system.

My interest developed in the context of an especially turbulent time in Arizona's history, defined by the passage of aggressive anti-immigrant laws and ordinances. One of these laws was SB1372, also known as the "Coyote Law". As a bill the law was lobbied by community and religious groups in collaboration with members of congress in an attempt to curtail the alleged growth of human smuggling violence in the state by establishing human smuggling as a crime. Some of the bill's advocates claimed powerful mafias of Mexican human smugglers (known in the region as coyotes or *polleros*) were behind the violent acts committed against irregular migrants in transit and called for the adoption of urgent measures against the "predators." The bill was approved into a law by the state congress and signed by the governor in August of 2005.

The creators of SB1372 hoped that the law would scare away smuggling groups and eventually reduce the incidence of human smuggling in the state. But only a few months after the law was signed, the Maricopa County attorney announced the wording of the law made no distinction between the actions of smugglers and the irregular migrants who hired their services. And starting in March of 2006, irregular migrants arrested while attempting to enter US territory began to be prosecuted under the law for their role in a conspiracy to commit an act of human smuggling—their own. By November of 2009, the law that had sought to decrease smuggling crimes in Arizona had led to the conviction of 1000 "co-conspirators."

As one of a handful of Spanish-speaking interviewers in my division, I was assigned to many of these conspiracy cases, which invariably involved irregular migrants not fluent in English. In fact, by late 2006, I was spending most of my time conducting investigations into human smuggling activities. It was while examining these cases that I began to notice that my interviewees' statements clashed with the court's perceptions surrounding human smuggling. Rather than referring to their journeys as criminal offenses, the men and women I interviewed spoke about their lives' goals and wishes, and how migration (albeit irregular) was a path toward accomplishing them. I heard about friendships and adventure; about determination, fear and hope. Their migratory journey, which to the eyes of the state amounted to a crime of human smuggling, constituted part of a much larger project of community and identity formation.

I was captivated by the experiences of my interviewees and their testimonies and their power. The social components of the migratory journey, as well as the interactions that developed among migrants, coyotes, friends and relatives, were abundant in meaning. But all along I was growing increasingly concerned about the state's processes that punished and criminalized their journeys without acknowledging the social contexts these journeys involved. Devoid of their social referents to friends, family, solidarity and trust, the reports that criminalized irregular migrants' journeys to *El Norte*[1] did not really seem to make much sense.

But the state was not interested in that subaltern "tale," as insightful as it could be. In fact, none of the sections of the presentence reports on human smuggling made reference to the context leading to the very migration for which the accused party (that is, the interviewee) had ultimately been arrested and charged. The court-ordered tests were more oriented at determining the detainees' likelihood to reoffend. Questions on actual migration experiences were hardly ever asked. No inquiries about the social dynamics present in the journey were conducted. And despite involving conspiracy charges, the actual interactions between the smuggler and their clients were consistently left out of the presentence report's narrative.

As I became aware of these gaps, I began to incorporate questions about migration and the border crossing journey. While conversations would many times start with a justification of migration as a response to financial need ("You see, the economic situation in Mexico is very bad . . . "), many others would simply start with a: "*Es que me dijeron que aca todo era bonito, y* yo *quise venir a ver*" ("I was told over here everything was pretty and *I* wanted to come see it"). Economic concerns rarely dominated our conversations. Instead, both men and women would go on to provide detailed and passionate accounts of their wish for new experiences, their longing for adventure or for opportunities to escape familial tensions or gendered constraints. By allowing them to narrate their own accounts rather than having them respond to specific questions, I was able to hear about people's aspirations to become "someone useful," to meet new people ("Perhaps even one of those artists that you see on TV?"), or to visit the distant places that other immigrants had seen before them. Those who had lived in the US in the past shared emotional accounts of the pain and fear that they experienced *following* their journeys. Others spoke of the sense of shame, isolation and loneliness that had at times characterized their experiences as migrants in the new country, as when Jose Benitez, a Mexican migrant, stated: "For 15 years I thought I was the only one who watched what I wore so that people didn't think I was a *mojarrita*."[2] But in all cases, migration was never described as the result of a cold economic calculation: it was about an individual's personal need for change—and growth.

It would be easy to assume that given the reasons behind their arrests—many of my interviewees had long histories of providing and relying on smuggling services—there would be a high reluctance among respondents to give details to a court officer about their cases. And yet, the majority spoke to me freely about their participation in human smuggling, mostly because the activity that the state had criminalized and deemed inherently exploitative and violent had actually enriched and changed their lives in ways they—and I—had never thought possible. In migrants' voices, smuggling was not a crime: it was a form of labor. But it was also a dignifying experience. It had given many the opportunity to provide for family; to secure a future (as abstract as the word "future" could be); and to fulfill life's simplest wishes—buy a pair of running shoes, a camera, a beaten up car; being able to afford dining at a restaurant, or going for a night out with friends.

Through each one of these interviews, I began to learn about the local smuggling market: about how it was constituted by loving single mothers, doting fathers, concerned friends and relatives and supportive neighbors, all working together to facilitate the transit of their friends and relatives into the country—not with a criminal intention but with the wish to help each other improve their economic condition and that of their families. I heard of how the feared smugglers had been migrants themselves, brought across the border by a coyote, and of the role their friends and families had played in their journeys. I also heard of how once in the US, an individual's inability to find employment or to remain employed during a particularly rough time had resulted in an invitation by concerned friends and family to participate in smuggling. I heard of the individual's gratitude over how this supplemental form of income allowed them to support their children or their families back home, of how smuggling had restored their confidence—and their dignity.

While for many of the men and women I interviewed their involvement in smuggling had indeed generated financial returns, they were more concerned with emphasizing the social and personal returns of their participation. Facilitating extra-legal border crossings had given sense to the lives of many, who until then—in their perception—had not been able to accomplish much else. And so instead of thinking of their actions as deviant—the way the state had defined them—smuggling facilitators were proud to be part of the reunification of children with their parents; of contributing to the joyful encounters among friends; or of arranging the one crossing that would save a human life—that of a diabetic patient unable to receive treatment in his or her country, or the one of a transsexual woman escaping hate and rejection.

This picture of smuggling as a community activity driven by solidarity strongly clashed with the official, pro-criminalization narratives of the state, where coyotes appeared as heinous monsters preying on the desperation and vulnerability of agency-deprived and manipulation-prone immigrants desperate to achieve the "American dream." During my entire experience within the court system, human smugglers were portrayed by the state as dark-skinned, apocalyptic transporters of human cargo invading the urban space; herds of insane decapitators running rampant across the nearby desert in broad daylight; rapists who wouldn't think twice about abandoning their victims to die. These characterizations troubled me, particularly when I knew none of them accurately portrayed the lives or the experiences of the many people I interviewed in jail everyday—even more when I became aware that erroneous, xenophobic and fear-loaded perceptions reduced the likelihood of my interviewees' chance for a fair, unbiased legal process.

My interactions with detainees and the clash of narratives involving smuggling operations created in me an urge to study the social dynamics of clandestine border crossings, but not from the criminalized stance I was forced to take as an employee of the state. Instead, I wanted to document the perspectives of the facilitators themselves. I wanted to write about the excitement, the happiness, the anger; the disappointment, the fear and even the love smuggling facilitators experienced in their everyday lives. I was convinced that these details, which perhaps were too trivial to be included in a court report, provided important clues into the social nature of smuggling.

Smuggling facilitators were not the only ones talking to me about their actions. Their perception as honest, reliable community members was shared by those who requested their services—the irregular migrants who were also prosecuted while under their care under the terms of the Coyote Law. Smuggling facilitators were described as highly regarded acquaintances, as friends valued for their honesty and support, and recognized for their roles as both negotiators and benefactors. And yet amid the fascination I felt for these accounts, I still had trouble understanding how these perspectives were so different from the graphic, gruesome characterizations of smuggling that continued to emerge with ever-growing euphoria in the media, which reinscribed stereotypical notions of smuggling facilitators as profit-driven, blood-thirsty *Mexican* criminals.

In my confusion, I also began to notice that the experience of interacting with smuggling facilitators was making me reexamine my own immigrant experience, helping me understand—or perhaps even complicate—much of its meaning. For a long time, I had questioned the neoclassic explanations of migration that described the phenomenon as nothing more than a reflex-like response to economic pressures or global income differentials—the kind theorized at length by some migration scholars and favored by the protestant, middle-class bootstraps' logic of the American mainstream. Academics had only been partially successful at theorizing the experiences of the migrants I knew. I was convinced that, in the lives of the men and women I interviewed, migration was much more than a mathematical calculation. I couldn't understand how concepts like happiness, excitement and joy did not figure in theorizations of migration, their experiences only described in the literature in terms of labor and production. I began to think of the possibility of conceiving migration as an act of resistance, of defiance, and personal change—the same way I had thought of my own.

And so I began to look for indicators of resistance and agency in the narratives of those whom I interviewed. It did not take me long to notice that, while the high demand for smuggling services had helped men and women in working as facilitators improve their finances, what they valued most was the degree of independence, empowerment and personal growth they had acquired through their experiences in smuggling. I also learned that migration was not always a response, as some migration scholars have proposed, to carefully calculated household economic strategies, but for many migrants it was a way to escape those very constraints and redefine them. I heard from women who crossed the border on their own to avoid having to support their younger siblings or parents, and of young men who, encouraged by the prospects of a single life without dependents, had headed North with the hope of learning more about themselves. None of these experiences had been conceptualized in the literature of migration I had seen thus far. In fact, the scholarship of migration I had read in graduate school was becoming increasingly ineffective at explaining how highly marginalized individuals could perceive their lives as a success despite their immensely limited circumstances. The interviews I conducted constituted mounting evidence that, despite the constraints they encountered, irregular migrants were engaged in a conscious effort to change and redefine their own identities and lives. And that they were proud of their achievements, regardless of the context in which they had taken place.

One of the main tenets of this study is that irregular migrants, despite their marginality and the limitations of their immigration status, develop mechanisms to improve the quality of their lives and that of their families that, while often reliant on their participation in illicit/criminalized markets, are considered as viable and legitimate forms of labor. I use the case of human smuggling to show how the participation of marginalized individuals in a highly criminalized activity does not inherently involve negative or criminal intentions. Instead, labor in the underground market of human smuggling allows migrants opportunities for self-growth and independence while creating new opportunities for other members of their same group to thrive. Human smuggling facilitators effectively navigate the constraints of their marginalization by fulfilling an essential need within an also marginal community: the need for unregulated mobility. Their involvement, and the very illicit nature of the activity, give in turn rise to normative behaviors that regulate facilitators' relationships and interactions with customers, friends, families and fellow facilitators which serve as a protective mechanism for all parties involved. The compliance of these norms allows not only for the continued survival of the smuggling market but for the generation of financial profits. Compliance further promotes and ensures social cohesion and creates new opportunities within the market for other people in need. I rely on smuggling facilitators' accounts of their activities to explore how their participation in the market allows them to create their social identity while ensuring the continuance of the market, but also contributing to their own personal development, as well as those of their customers via their migration.

This study aims to understand how involvement in alternative markets constitutes an opportunity for marginalized individuals to achieve a sense of independence and personal advancement within the very socio-legal system that works at limiting their social, economic and legal mobility. At the same time, and while cognizant of the potential for violence of illicit markets, the goal of the study is not to highlight the degree of victimization immigrants are likely to face in their everyday lives, like other studies on border dynamics have shown, but rather to show how illicit markets like smuggling provide opportunities for the exercise of agency through immigrants' adaptation and resistance in a highly constrained context.

My decision to "migrate"

Having decided to conduct research on the dynamics of the men and women who facilitate irregular migrants' travels, I began to seek opportunities that would grant me access to the smuggling market. Initially—and naïvely—I shared my research intentions with the very people I interviewed, not really sure about their reaction. Virtually every single one of the people I spoke to volunteered to assist me and even offered to get me in contact with other smuggling facilitators willing to share their experiences. But given my position as a state employee, the possibility of conducting ethnographic work involving an extremely criminalized activity – and an exceptionally vulnerable population—was virtually off the table from the onset (although the fear of being dismissed from the must fulfilling job I had ever had was greater than that of being accused or even charged with conspiring to commit smuggling activities). But having also shared my research interests with colleagues and law enforcement officers, I was afforded incredible opportunities to witness and document human smuggling operations in the field—or at least, as they took place.

One of these opportunities involved participating in a wiretap investigation of a group of smuggling facilitators operating in Phoenix. From the onset, I was immediately fascinated by the richness of the everyday interactions among the group's members, the alliances and agreements that guided their activities, the ethics and values that regulated their exchanges with other groups and with the immigrants they served. I reconfirmed how aspects like violence, friendship and the presence – or absence—of romantic relationships among coyotes, their customers and third parties seemed to carry more meaning than investigators—none of whom spoke Spanish—could realize.

When after a few days I naïvely decided to share my observations with the law enforcement officers involved in the case, I found out the focus of investigations like these was never to develop an understanding of smuggling's dynamics, but simply to arrest as many "operators" as possible. I remember leaving the wire room feeling angry and humiliated, sensing my observations had probably been seen as puerile. But mostly I was saddened by the realization that investigations of this nature would most likely lead to the arrests of the many men and women to whose conversations I had religiously listened. I couldn't avoid the feeling of guilt that invaded me, and I walked away from the wiretap experiment.

Following my initial disappointment, I later realized the wiretap experience had been invaluable. It provided me with a laboratory to validate many of my hypotheses about the social dynamics of smuggling operations. And by listening to the experiences of the facilitators as they occurred, I gained an even better understanding of how normative behaviors emerged and developed in the smuggling market.

As time went by, my research interests became a bit more complex. I became critical of the actions involving the state, especially in the context of the growing numbers of measures to criminalize even more aspects of immigrants' lives in Arizona. I was also growing painfully aware that, despite my best intentions, my position as a court interviewer did little to generate any awareness involving what I considered to be the real face of smuggling operations—let alone generate any kind of social change. Furthermore, I was all along aware of my role as an agent of the very state which actions I had become critical of, and of my inability to help the men and women I interviewed in that capacity.

In July of 2007 I decided to quit my job with the Superior Court to start a doctoral program where I could research border crossing operations and their criminalization at the hands of the state. In a sense, my decision involved a form of migration—I was leaving the comfortable, familiar settings of the courthouse for the unknown world of academia.

My familiarity with coyotes and smuggling had, however, a very different origin. While my academic interest in human smuggling operations was born as a result of my experience in Superior Court, it was also tied to my own experiences as a migrant. I was raised in a Mexican peasant family with a long history of US-bound migration (my grandfather, a railroad worker, lived as a *Bracero*[3] in Northern California from 1938 to 1943). The majority of my male relatives have in fact migrated at some point in their lives to the United States, often as irregular migrants, as well as an ever-growing number of aunts, female cousins and nieces. I am myself a migrant, having left Mexico as a teenager. But since my migration took place under extremely privileged circumstances— I was fortunate enough to travel with a valid passport and visa—my experience was for the longest time not considered a "true" act of migration by many of my relatives. My journey had been, in their words, "too easy." Given that most of my female relatives' border crossings had involved the assistance of smuggling facilitators, I was never afforded the opportunity to claim what I perceived as a community-sanctioned, full-fledged migrant status. After all, I had not experienced the negotiations leading to my travel; I did not know of the endless bus rides to the border, or of the anxious wait to cross *La Linea*[4] at night. Even my grandparents' own experience of dealing with my departure did not seem to carry the same weight in the eyes of other parents whose children had migrated. They did not have to come up with my smuggling fee, nor experience the agony of the long silence between my departure and arrival—the dreaded hours waiting for a coyote to confirm a positive border crossing outcome. And so even after having lived in the United States for several years, I always felt that in a sense I had to prove to my family that my experience amounted to the "real thing."

In the fall of 1999, I was detained by immigration authorities in Arizona while trying to re-enter the US following a brief stay in Mexico, when an officer inspecting my bags found my student identification card. Believing, as many migrants do, that by being honest the *migra*[5] would simply let me go, I proudly explained that, despite having no "papers,"[6] I was enrolled in university in San Francisco. I went on to tell the officer how I hoped to eventually get a degree in anthropology. And suspecting he would appreciate full disclosure, I also admitted that I was working without employment authorization.

My confession earned me 13 days in immigration detention.

Until that moment, and perhaps as a result of the cultural silencing that characterized the migrant experiences of my hometown's female relatives and friends, I had always assumed that migration "troubles" of the kind I had gotten myself into were something that was only meant to be lived by men. And so, as I was being escorted handcuffed to the back of an immigration service truck, I felt shame, wondering how my arrest would be described to (and blamed upon) my grandparents, for having allowed me—a woman—to migrate on her own.

To my disbelief, there were no men in that truck. Every single person in the back of the *perrera*⁷ was female. The same happened at the detention centers in Arizona, North Las Vegas and San Diego where I was eventually taken. And perhaps fueled by the feeling of anonymity surrounding our detention ("After all, you and I know we'll never see each other again," a young pregnant woman told me), incarceration created an ideal space for sharing.

It was here where I had my first encounter with smuggling facilitators, who unlike the male coyotes behind my relatives' journeys were women. Women had worked as coyotes facilitating the crossing of other migrants into the US simply to do a favor, and only occasionally in exchange for payment. They spoke about the numerous challenges they faced in a male-dominated business; of the conflicts emerging among working partners and sometimes among competitors; of their past experiences crossing children or families; of the ways they understood their actions; of their wish to help others in need—men and women like themselves who had turned to smuggling to improve their lives.

Most of the women I spent those days with were only waiting for deportation orders and knew that the possibility of entering the US would become even more remote as a result of their arrest. I was aware—and at times ashamed—of my privilege. I had a passport. And a visa. It was only a matter of time before I was released from immigration custody facing no charges or sanctions, and a few months later I was on my path to citizenship. Once my immigration status changed, I was allowed to re-enroll in school and I eventually went on to graduate with the anthropology degree I so proudly spoke to the officer about. But the memories of my time in immigration detention, my crucial migrant upbringing and my experience interviewing migrants facing criminal charges were all central elements in my decision to research extralegal border crossings and their criminalization by the state.

Chasing the "smugglers"

My interest in the study of human smuggling and extralegal border crossing practices has been further informed and shaped by three realizations. First, and even before entering the doctoral program, I was troubled by the minimal attention migration scholarship had paid to the very journeys that transform people into migrants. In part, I attributed this oversight to the fact that the study of the transit involving irregular migrants—the providers of low-skilled, low-paying labor—generated less interest than that paid to the experiences of professional or skilled immigrants, whose assimilation and economic mobility are frequently at the core of the discussions on entrepreneurship and industrial innovation. Moreover, while the events of 9/11 generated a wave of publications on smuggling operations, most analyses centered on the impact of smuggling on national security and border protection, both concerns of the nation-state. In either case, I considered the lack of attention paid by US immigration scholars to the dynamics leading to what is considered one of the largest and continuous migrations between any two countries in the contemporary world an issue that needed to be addressed.

A second realization involved the troubling sensationalism surrounding the rhetoric on smuggling operations in Arizona which has gone hand in hand with the anti-immigrant sentiment in the state. To date, the state's discourse on smuggling continues to be plagued by unsubstantiated claims portraying coyotes as indomitable, violent, drugged, hyper-predatory Mexican males who consort with Mexican drug trafficking organizations in their attempts to dominate the state's landscape (Hensley 2011; Francis 2008; Miller 2011; Nill-Sanchez 2010). While the severe incidents involving the victimization of irregular migrants at the hands of some crossing facilitators constitute a valid reason for concern, the coverage surrounding smuggling is highly problematic due to its xenophobic, racialized tones. The official discourse has done little to improve the understanding of smuggling operations in the state and has further complicated the dynamics of race relations in Arizona.

Lastly, I saw the need to learn from immigrants' own accounts about their involvement in alternative cash-generating strategies that promote not only economic profits, but viable opportunities for personal development by engaging in what they consider a legitimate form of labor. My exposure to critical race theory and to the study of feminism and gender, and the accounts of the many immigrants I have been fortunate to interview over the years provided me with a platform from which to approach irregular border crossings as constituting a form of knowledge that had to be explored.

Data sources

This project is based on the qualitative analysis of 66 cases of men and women, aged 18 and over, charged with human smuggling and human smuggling-related offenses committed in Maricopa County, Arizona in the period comprised between March of 2006 and January of 2011. All cases selected for this study involve convictions under SB1372, the Arizona criminal statute which eventually became known as the "Coyote Law" because of its intended use in the prosecution of human smuggling facilitators. Under SB1372, smuggling facilitators as well as the irregular migrants who purchase their services can be—and have been— charged with committing an act of human smuggling, despite the differences in their roles.

I also relied on a series of one-on-one informal, open-ended interviews with smuggling facilitators, their families and clients on their personal migratory journeys and their experiences on irregular migration and smuggling. These interviews were primarily used for hypothesis validation and data verification purposes, and constituted an invaluable source of information that allowed me to tie up loose ends, clarify doubts and confirm processes, practices and patterns. It is through these informants' voices, and through those also present in the legal record, that the social and community nature of smuggling operations took life.

In addition, I performed participant observation within and around several locations in the Phoenix metropolitan area (such as restaurants, beauty parlors, money-wiring businesses, food stands, bars, parking lots of detention facilities and open-air markets) where I held formal and informal conversations with individuals who had been involved in some aspect of smuggling, either as border crossers or as facilitators. During my research, I was able to develop a network of friends, acquaintances and casual informants with whom I spoke about the social practices involved in border crossings, focusing primarily on the personal meanings of their experiences in the market, either as coyotes or as travelers.

While some of these research interactions were more formal than others, the majority were the result of happenstance. For example, I often found myself striking up conversations with strangers at food stands in downtown Phoenix late at night. Many of the people I spoke with were aware that the chance of us meeting again under similar circumstances was small. Many provided key answers to interpret missing or faulty data, and some offered additional help if I had any other questions. A couple of people even indicated that I could contact them if I were ever in need of crossing assistance myself (an offer I never had the opportunity to accept).

Throughout the whole process, participants proved essential at clarifying the gaps arising from my analysis of the case files, while the case files themselves yielded details of which the participants were unaware or were perhaps unwilling to discuss openly. As my research continued, the data began to reveal the existence of a rather amorphous community organized into extended households or in small groups of friends who would occasionally work together to facilitate extralegal border crossings from the US–Mexico border into Phoenix's surrounding cities and neighborhoods. Those involved were mostly connected to each other by virtue of kinship or friendship, and shared the highways and back roads leading to Maricopa County, their cell phones, cars and homes, to assist irregular border crossers in their transits into Phoenix, from where they could hire additional transportation services to other in-country destinations with the assistance of other facilitators or by collaborating with other border crossers.

The men and women I interviewed were the feared smugglers of Maricopa County, the details of their lives absent from politicians' speeches or the stories presented on the evening news. They attended church on Sundays, celebrated their children's birthday parties and occasionally placed bets at the cockfights. They enjoyed soccer, hated doing business with family and valued hard-working collaborators. They worried about their ability to pay rent and supported their families on a regular salary (most were employed, and too many held more than one job). And most were irregular migrants themselves, what made them deeply concerned about the anti-immigrant climate in Arizona and the implications of immigration enforcement upon their families' lives. In short, the human smuggling facilitators I met were ordinary people, residing in a community where their presence had historically been vilified, and whose income-generating choices combined with the precariousness of their immigration status had made them the target of the anti-immigrant policies of the state.

An additional note on access

During the fieldwork and data collection period, I identified myself as a student. Many of the men and women who assisted me in my research were intrigued by my interest in the social dynamics of smuggling and some even questioned the relevance of smuggling as a research subject, asking, "*Y a poco eso se estudia?*"[8] I did not use deception, always informing those willing to share their testimonies on border crossing of the academic nature of my work. Being a student actually proved useful, as many conversations delved into facilitators' own perceptions of education and the educational hopes they had for their children, most of whom were US citizens. Carrying books and legal case files into the places where I conducted participant observation or occasionally sat for lunch also led to conversations and even to people volunteering unsolicited information. Cynthia, one of my most trusted collaborators—a respected coordinator of border crossings with valuable connections and an impeccable reputation, who had been married to a well-known local coyote for 10 years, and was in the process of "quitting" smuggling after becoming the girlfriend of a high-ranking local US Border Patrol officer—was in fact the one who approached me to ask about my research, concerned over the amount of time I spent reading field notes whenever I visited her beauty salon.

Over the years I have interviewed hundreds of migrants, refugees and those behind their journeys about their border crossing experiences along the migratory trails in Mexico, the US, Costa Rica, Morocco, Tunis, Palestine, Iraq and Australia. What has surprised me the most about people's testimonies are the striking similarities in their smuggling experiences across countries as diverse as these. These exchanges have taught me, as Vélez-Ibáñez says, "much about history and ways of thinking, but especially about the courage of people fighting to survive" (1996, 6). In this sense, my fieldwork has allowed me to witness the execution of increasingly intrusive and punitive systems of hyper-vigilance and controls across borders by the state, but, most importantly, migrants and refugees' everyday efforts at maintaining their dignity.

Why do smugglers talk about smuggling?

It would be amiss to explain the access that I gained to human smuggling facilitators and their families on the basis of ethnicity, community ties and happenstance alone. The openness with which participants spoke during the course of this research was also a consequence of the very nature of extralegal border crossings. While these are illicit in nature, they are socially accepted in the context of the historical processes involving labor demand, the culture of migration between Mexico and the US and the day-to-day dynamics of a border region that has over time been excluding and violent toward the racialized "other"—in this case,

Latinos, particularly those of Mexican origin. The work performed by smuggling facilitators is collectively understood as one, if not the only, mechanism available to those unable to obtain the recognition of the state through visas or crossing permits to cross borders. In this context, human smuggling emerges as an example of how "the state and the formal economy through sanctions and regulations" imposed upon mobility have created the conditions whereby illegal and informal ways of working (that is, activities like human smuggling) become normalized (Galemba, 2008, 22). Human smuggling facilitators therefore operate within a continuum of legality and illegality, one that establishes them as criminal in front of the state, but which also situates them, especially in the eyes of those who have been stripped of their right to mobility by the state, as the only viable means of ensuring their transits—and sometimes even their survival.

The people I interviewed never spoke of their involvement in criminal terms, perhaps since my questioning never sought to explore the criminal nature of such activities, but instead focused on the dynamics of their daily lives.[9] As Chapter 4 will explain, the everyday challenges faced by smuggling facilitators are quite similar to those associated with many other occupations. Stress, anxiety and boredom are common. There are frequent arguments among family members, and many disputes remain unresolved simply to keep the peace. While my awareness of smuggling based on my professional and personal experiences taught me to never ask for personal information or specific names— these would often be shared during the conversation regardless, most of the time completely unsolicited—most participants simply wanted to vent. Veteran or seasoned smugglers were an endangered species, with most becoming tired of the increasingly low returns and a clientele whose ethics, in their opinion, no longer merited trust.

This was the way I eventually found myself spending long Saturday afternoons in detention facilities, parks, church halls and restaurants, involved in conversations not with the sanguinary predators the media and my supervisors had warned me about, but with ordinary men and women who reflected on failed relationships, domestic violence and personal health concerns; who had high hopes for their children and their futures; who were frequently disgusted by the anti-immigrant sentiment plaguing Arizona; and who feared that this sentiment—and not their involvement in smuggling—would ultimately be the cause of their arrest. Their personal stories, including their role in facilitating border crossings, form the core of this book.

The language of borders, the language of smuggling

As Adele Jones explains, "typologies of migration—economic, forced, displacement, exile, asylum, undocumented, and trafficking—like the phenomena they seek to describe, are subject to dominant political forces and hegemonic discourses" (2008, 762). As a fundamental element of immigration regimes, the terms coined within these typologies in turn label the undesirable, further facilitating their criminalization and subjection to specific forms of marginalization, including violence. Jones further states:

> that the official language of migration is inextricably wedded to popular discourses that frame migrants in pathologizing ways is well documented . . . the parallel market in which the currency of migration terms circulates, reveals implicit racialized and gendered codes that serve to separate out a nation's outsiders from those "legally" entitled to the nation's protection.
>
> (Davies 1996; Jones 2001, quoted in Jones 2008, 762)[10]

Aside from the already discussed portrayal of human smuggling as dangerous or predatory within national security and scholarly discourses, the term "smuggling" itself has been relied upon to frame the border crossing experiences of migrants and refugees as illicit in a way that leaves the smuggler limited room to redefine a role other than that already characterized by violence, greed and exploitation. The predatory nature of smuggling facilitators is simply taken for granted.

Yet in direct opposition to paternalistic and disciplinarian discourses of protection and control, there is a lexicon associated with extralegal border crossings developed by migrants, refugees and smugglers that is creative, complex and rhetorically rich in nature (Spener 2009b). This language emerges directly from the day-to-day interactions among these actors, and opens the possibility of exploring the meanings embedded within their border crossing practices. The most well-known example is the use of the word "coyote" to collectively designate the men and women who facilitate extralegal border crossings. The term, which draws from Mesoamerican traditions that characterized this canine as cunning and mischievous, has in fact been used historically throughout Mexico and Central America to refer to those who conduct cumbersome and time-consuming bureaucratic tasks on behalf of others for a fee, often illicitly (Valle 2005). The word has been used to such an extent that it has been appropriated by US law enforcement agencies, incorporated into their lexicon to refer to human smuggling facilitators in official documents.[11]

And yet, while smuggling facilitators are aware of the use of specific terminology in reference to their activities, they often opt not to identify themselves by it, often denouncing the use of the term coyote itself. In fact, during my fieldwork, multiple facilitators rejected that designation and requested to be called by their first names. On one occasion I witnessed a coordinator (those in charge of organizing the logistics of a border crossing) ask a potential client to refer to him by his nickname, *Chato*, but never coyote. "If you can avoid it, do not call me coyote because that I am not," he remarked.

While Chato's reticence to be called a coyote could be interpreted as a precautionary measure—facilitators operate with a certain degree of secrecy, being well aware of the fact that their phone conversations are frequently monitored by law enforcement—it might also reflect facilitators' understanding of their role in the smuggling market. The use of the word coyote seems to indicate a level of professionalization with which most facilitators in this sample were not willing to align. And so while many of the men and women I interviewed echoed Chato's request, they also asked to emphasize the role they each performed (such as driver, lookout, walker or cook), never describing their activities as those of a coyote.

Given the participants' objection to their designation as coyotes, and the stigma often associated with the word (as a result of the vilification of smugglers in the context of a criminalized border, and their alleged connections to organized crime), in this project I make every effort to refer to them by the name they selected at the time of their interview. When no name was provided (as in the case of testimonies drawn directly from legal case files), one was assigned at random. Despite the prevalence of the word coyote in connection to extralegal border crossings along the US–Mexico border, but primarily in light of participants' reticence to be identified as coyotes, I rely on the term to describe these actors only sparingly and only when collectively referring to them.

I also rely on the term "facilitator" to designate those involved in the provision of smuggling services, in what I acknowledge constitutes a rather limited attempt to reduce the connotation of the term "smuggler," which tends to reinscribe the criminality of the men and women behind migrant and refugee journeys. I am fully aware of the limitations posed by both terms, and opted for the one that in my opinion suggested a more collaborative nature. Further, I use the term "extralegal border crossing" to refer to the transit services facilitators provide and their unregulated nature. Along those lines, while I use the term irregular migrant, I often rely on the phrase "border crosser" when referring to those who rely on the services of facilitators. The reason for this choice is twofold: not all of those who cross the border seek to migrate, and the emphasis on migrants has historically excluded a significant segment of people who also rely on smuggling services, namely, asylum seekers (a population that, according to some non-governmental organizations [NGOs], is growing in size among those seeking to cross the US–Mexico border extralegally) (See Reynolds 2014). A variation of the term—irregular border crosser, or IRB—was initially coined by Rubio-Goldsmith and her team (2006) in the context of their work on deaths along the Arizona migration corridor. This last term has also proven significant as it recognizes (as Pickering and Weber identify with their use of "illegalized traveler") "the legal and political power of those who define who is to be included and who excluded at the border," and represents "the political and legal discourses that define representations of legal and illegal actors" (Weber and Pickering 2011, 4).

Justification

Maricopa County was chosen as a research site for several reasons. First, the in-county support for state-sponsored anti-immigrant practices, many of which have resulted in federal quests into the violation of Latinos' human and civil rights (see Romero and Serag 2005; Campbell 2011; US Department of Justice, 2012). Two of the most recognized examples of these practices are SB1070, which placed

Arizona at the center of an international controversy over the state's endorsement of racial profiling practices, and SB1372, the Coyote Law at the center of smuggling operations.

A second factor was the role Maricopa County Sheriff's Office (MCSO) has played in enforcing local immigration law. Through local policing practices like employment-site raids and the setting up of checkpoints in sections of town with large Latino presence, MCSO has been effective at terrorizing Latino families in the county and restricting their free transit, limiting their civic and political participation.

Maricopa County was also an ideal site to conduct this research in light of its role as one of the US's top human smuggling hubs. As described in Chapter 2, since the late 1990s and largely as a result of the implementation of federal immigration control initiatives along the US–Mexico border, Arizona had by the mid-2000s become the main point of entry for irregular migrants into the US. Maricopa County, and the Phoenix Metropolitan Area in particular, provides access to an exceptional network of roads and highways connecting the state to other regions in the country. These routes are believed to have facilitated the consolidation of Maricopa County as one of the country's main undocumented immigration hubs by facilitating the fast transportation of irregular migrants.

Despite its geographic and political importance, no other studies looking into the operations of human smuggling facilitators in Arizona have been conducted, which underscores the need for the study. Furthermore, despite their role in facilitating the transit of irregular migrants, only a handful of studies have been conducted on the operation of human smugglers in the United States.

Aims

This book seeks:

- To understand the dynamics of human smuggling operations in Maricopa County from the perspective of the irregular migrants who participate in them as facilitators. With this goal in mind I analyze the accounts of the everyday activities on the inside of smuggling groups to outline their social organization and structure, in an attempt to understand the interactions that carry social meaning to facilitators, meanings which are in turn transmitted to the inside of the group and to the customers the groups serve.
- To demystify sensationalized, unsubstantiated and stereotyped understandings of border crossing operations, which to date have been primarily based on largely anecdotal and journalistic evidence. The official narratives involving smuggling define it as a criminal activity carried out by well-organized, armed and violent gangs of Mexican citizens. By systematically analyzing the accounts provided by smuggling facilitators themselves, the study points to the inaccuracies of the official interpretations. And by privileging the voices of smuggling facilitators' and their customers, smuggling activities become legitimate sources of data in the social dynamics of underground economies.

- To understand the social and political consequences of immigration law enforcement in Maricopa County. This is accomplished by analyzing law enforcement policing practices established as a response to smuggling events.
- To contribute to the scholarship of migration by providing an analysis of an under-studied yet essential aspect of the migratory experience and thereby removing the mystery and sensationalism that surrounds human smuggling activities.

Organization

This book approaches smuggling operations as community-based activities facilitated by irregular migrants of similar ethnic backgrounds, working in loosely organized groups to facilitate undetected border crossings. Most smuggling groups operate with no criminal intention, and seek instead to generate financial, but also personal development opportunities for all participants involved and for their social circles.

Chapter 1 addresses the enterprise and organization of human smuggling as reported by its actors—the men and women charged with facilitating the activity in the context of the smuggling literature. The chapter provides a model to understand the structural characteristics of smuggling, as well as its organizational dimensions like membership, leadership and power, structural flexibility and adaptability.

Chapter 2 presents an analysis of anti-smuggling enforcement practices in a historical context. I suggest that state practices have throughout history created the conditions for structural inequality that have disproportionally impacted communities of color in Arizona. This chapter also delves into the use of racial profiling practices, and to the overall intimidation women and children are subjected in the context of smuggling investigations.

Chapter 3 delves into the everyday experiences of smuggling facilitators. It addresses—unlike criminal investigations seeking to map the "motives" behind "involvement"—the emergence of smuggling along communities in Arizona as an effort on the part of immigrants to generate supplementary income strategies for their immediate circles of friends and families through the creation of occasional employment opportunities.

Chapter 4 describes the nature of the interactions between smuggling facilitators and their customers. It explores how this relationship goes beyond the existence of economic interests, and is in fact based on deep, socially-cemented ties spanning across countries.

Chapter 5 explores the experiences of women as human smuggling facilitators, and reveals how, in a highly gendered market like smuggling, women have carved a niche by providing services perceived to increase the safety and protection of the most vulnerable—services that also carry gendered implications for women and their families.

Chapter 6 takes a structural approach to understanding smuggling-related violence, situating it as an element of the continuum of violence immigrants are likely to face during the course of their migratory experience, embedded in state practices and exercised by multiple actors—not smugglers alone.

Lastly, the closing section provides a brief conclusion of the findings, contributions and limitations of this project.

Notes

1 The North.
2 Irregular migrant.
3 The Bracero Program allowed Mexican nationals to take temporary work in the United States. During the program's 22-year life, more than 4.5 million Mexican nationals were legally contracted for work in the United States.
4 The Border.
5 Immigration officer.
6 Legal authorization to reside in the country.
7 Name given to US Border Patrol vehicles used to carry unauthorized border crossers.
8 "Is this an actual topic of study?"
9 This approach echoes that adopted by Philip Bourgois in his work among crack vendors in New York's Spanish Harlem, documented in the book *In Search of Respect: Selling Crack in the Barrio.*
10 In the current lexicon of the American migratory imagination, for example, the use of terms like "illegal" and "anchor baby" carries deeply racial and gendered connotations, the first typically being used to designate undocumented Latino migrants, while the latter reinscribes not only the notion of Latina women as having a preternatural ability to reproduce (Chavez 2013) but also their Machiavellian goal of crossing the border surreptitiously in order to deliver babies that eventually will earn them the much "prized" US citizenship.
11 It is not uncommon to come across official legal documents that include references made by officers and legal/court staff to smuggling facilitators as coyotes and to irregular migrants in detention as *pollos* (chickens). This suggests the incorporation—or rather appropriation—of the language of clandestine migration into the official accounts of the authorities in charge of policing borders.

1 On borders, smugglers and the imagination

The border between the United States of America (US) and Mexico occupies a central place in the imaginarium of both countries. It does not merely constitute the political line that separates them. Deemed a dangerous place plagued by criminals, sin and vice, the region has historically been sneered at by both Mexicans and Americans. Americans have learnt to conceive it as the virginal land ravaged by the incursion of hordes of irregular migrants; the main point of entry for weapons, drugs, stolen human organs and even terrorists; as the land of brothels, erotic indiscretions and liquor. To Mexicans, the border is the decrepit place where the nation ceases to exist. It is not by coincidence that in Mexico it is colloquially referred to as *El Bordo*: the last frontier, the edge of the land. It is a place dominated by lawlessness, where the *narco* reigns, where women are destined to a life of prostitution and where the *ilegal*—the nation's quintessential pariah—goes to die. It is a geographic accident, a repulsive fissure and the revolting creatures that inhabit it.

Many scholars of the contemporary US–Mexico border have primarily approached it as a lethal place, transforming it into both the subject and the location of countless efforts to quantify the ever-growing number of human casualties resulting from failed immigration and border control policies. Yet efforts emphasizing the humanitarian crisis in irregular migration along this border have often led to the decontextualized, ahistorical treatment of the everyday lives of the communities who call it home. This has rendered invisible people's daily exchanges with the state, including their struggles for survival (Romero 2006; Vélez-Ibáñez 1996). While the policing practices that maintain and reinforce the subordinate status of marginalized groups along borders have been the subject of much examination, the ways in which the people of the border resist and redefine the limits of their marginalization have often been absent in official accounts and academic analysis.

It is therefore not surprising that, despite their historical presence along the border, discussions on the roles of the men and women who facilitate extralegal border crossings across this geopolitical divide—known in criminology as human smugglers, and colloquially along the US–Mexico border as coyotes or *polleros* – have been mostly absent from the policy and academic conversations on the border, unless when depicted as the predatory, violent *men* who take advantage of the naïveté and desperation of the thousands of migrants seeking an opportunity to cross. Within this narrative, human smugglers have become the quintessential villains in a time of failed attempts at border control, shifting migration flows and the deterritorialization of the border space. They are often characterized in media and policy circles as members of transnational organized crime groups, peons— or lords—of hierarchical structures, driven by greed and the promise of untold profits.[1] Policy reports describe them as conniving and cruel, prone to abandoning their victims along scorching deserts, to raping virginal maidens, even to stealing children—for satanic rituals at worst and for the illegal adoption market at best (US District Court v. Mirtha Veronica Nava-Martinez 2013; Bowe 2007).

Despite the abundance of graphic characterizations and sensationalist coverage surrounding the activities of those involved in the facilitation of extralegal border crossings, empirical evidence on them is scant. This absence is even more notorious in relation to the US–Mexico border—ground zero of one of the largest, continual migrations between two countries in contemporary history and one which historically has been dominated by images of illegality, precarious journeys, crime and death.

Contemporary work on the US–Mexico border has looked at the policy issues concerning the role of structural violence and has extensively documented the violence experienced by those who call the border home, as well as those who seek to cross it. And yet the border crossing journey as a mechanism of migration, the experiences of border crossers and the role of human smugglers as facilitators of that journey are, with a few exceptions or within a specific rhetoric, forgotten themes in the scholarship on the border, most research on US-bound migration focusing on documenting the experiences of migrants already living within American society, largely ignoring the importance of the transit and arrival processes.

The absence of the smuggler as a facilitator of mobility is also evident in the global scholarship on migration. Uncountable academic inquiries have delved into the migratory processes of assimilation and acculturation, documenting the lives of irregular migrants and asylum seekers once they have arrived at what is often presumed to be their destination. Critical criminology has been fundamental in exploring migrants' and refugees' experiences in detention, and the challenges they face amid immigration regimes and the overall criminalization of migration (Pickering 2014; Heyman 2013; Chacon 2012; Bosworth and Kauffman 2011). Yet most efforts at mapping human mobility flows of an irregular or extralegal nature have either ignored the role of smuggling facilitators or only incorporated the most extreme of their characterizations in analyses of migration and mobility (Zhang 2009; Agustín 2006, 2007).

The rhetoric that characterizes human smugglers as violent and callous has been effective at generating awareness of their existence—a presence that has been primarily connected to tragedies involving the death or near-death experiences of migrants and refugees. The magnitude of these tragic events has in turn been effective at sparking the public's moral outrage against human smuggling, albeit temporarily (Carr 2013). Yet few of these well-intentioned efforts engage upon critical analyses of what the presence of foreigners traveling irregularly suggests: the inability of millions of people worldwide to access a legal path to mobility, due to efforts on the part of the nation-state to control and protect borders.

In an effort to examine the discourses of human smuggling along borders, this project shifts the attention away from the spectacle of suffering toward an analysis of those frequently portrayed as its perpetrators. This book focuses on one of the most objectified and vilified characters of migration processes: the human smuggler. This work is based on the testimonies of smugglers themselves, who historically have been perceived by those seeking to cross borders as highly valued agents of mobility. Human smugglers worldwide are relied upon to facilitate the migration of women and children trying to reunite with their families, to coordinate the transit of refugees and asylum seekers, to transport those too sick or too weak to move, and to assist in the crossings of the many others for whom legal paths to cross geopolitical divides are simply inaccessible. While millions rely on these services, little is known about smuggler operations, social dynamics or organization. Even less is known about facilitators' day-to-day lives outside of smuggling.

This project therefore constitutes an effort to "restore dignity to the environment[s] of the region, and agency to an otherwise objectified and ignored people" (Insley 2004, 100) whose actions are central to the migration process but whose experiences have been silenced in the context of a border dominated by narratives of national security, death and crime. This is a book about coyotes in Arizona—ground zero of the contemporary American debate on immigration, and the main point of entry for irregular migrants in the US, one of the country's primary human smuggling centers.

This chapter explores the narratives connected to the smuggler as a global predator and their rationale. It raises questions over the characterizations that so far have dominated the discourse of smuggling, which more than often have been driven by graphic characterizations of suffering women and children of color, lacking contextualization. The chapter also explores the theoretical and empirical contexts of smuggling scholarship and highlights the importance of Arizona in the US immigration control debate, prior to the next chapter's discussion on this state's immigration legislation and its impact.

The human smuggler as a global predator

The mere mention of "human smuggler" generates an immediate series of frightful images. Online or media searches on human smuggling reveal gruesome stories of dark-skin Mexicans who abandon their victims in deserts (Rose 2012); of cruel Muslim pirates who force their own women and children off ferries and boats into the ocean (Al-Hajj 2008); of rapists whose uncontrollable sex drive condemns *young* and *female* victims to the calvary of sex trafficking (Kunambura 2014); and of the white saviors who rescue them (Constable 2014). These racialized, gendered and morally loaded representations of smuggling not only reinscribe notions of men of color as violent and sexually deviant, and of migrant and refugee women and children from the global south as in need of salvation; they are also effective at categorizing the human smuggler as being single-handedly responsible for the deaths of thousands of migrants and asylum seekers along the global frontiers (Weber and Pickering 2011).

Inquests into human smuggling have also prioritized the rhetoric of the practice as being under the control of large, transnational, highly complex and economically powerful criminal organizations that rely on violence to extract financial profits from their victims (UNODC 2011; IOM 2011). Portrayals are not only effective at justifying increases in the levels of policing and surveillance along and beyond borders and the accompanying criminalization of mobility, but further obscure the importance of exploring the reasons behind the continued reliance of migrants and refugees on extralegal border crossing services—namely the lack of access to visas and passports—positioning smugglers as solely responsible for the human tragedies involving extralegal journeys.

In academia, the role of the human smuggler—and that of extralegal border crossings as elements of mobility—has been the subject of scant theoretical and empirical inquiry. While the representation of the human smuggler as embodied culprit and modern folk devil in official narratives of migration has been widely recognized by scholars (see Weber and Pickering 2011, 164; Weber and Grewcock 2011), smugglers' roles as agents of mobility have remained largely unexamined. Instead it is common to come across scholarly pieces on migration that recirculate the popular depiction of smuggling facilitators as greedy, violent and inhumane predators of the weak, further inscribing them as perpetrators of the power which they allegedly command, subjected to virtually no scrutiny or rationalization.

Despite the pervasive presence of tragic stories surrounding smugglers, and the precariousness associated with irregular border crossings, the demand of smuggling services is constant. Reports of the successful, even if accidented, arrivals of thousands of irregular migrants and refugees to distant destinations, amid occasional stories of tragedies, serve as constant reminders not only of people's determination to travel despite the risks involved, but of the reliance on smuggling facilitators and their effectiveness.

Among those who travel without state protections, human smugglers are often perceived not as predators, but rather as providing a significant, if not the only, layer of protection (Ahmad 2011; Zhang 2007; Spener 2009b; Hagan 2008). Travel with smugglers is known to reduce the risks and the likelihood of detection, arrest, victimization and abuse (see Izcara-Palacios 2012a, 2012b). Messages that depict smugglers as dangerous and rapacious have scant impact, the smuggler consistently perceived as benevolent, and as a legitimate provider of trans-border safety.[2]

The widespread confidence in smuggling among those who travel irregularly also suggests that the imposition of barriers to keep the unwanted outside the walls of the state has only consolidated the need for and reliance on an alternative, assisted means of mobility (one that, far from being feared or distrusted, provides a sense of safeguard and increases the likelihood of successfully reaching a destination). In other words, as Weber and Grewcock (2011) have argued, it is the barriers to mobility which have allowed for the emergence of the smuggling market, and at the same time irregular migrants and asylum seekers continue to rely on the services of facilitators of extralegal journeys, guided not by fear of rape, death or deception, but instead seeking effective ways to ameliorate the impact of violence and danger inherent to policing and surveillance along borders.

The literature on smuggling

Despite the abundance of references to the abuses of smuggling facilitators, their role in transnational organized crime and even their ties to terrorist networks, only a few empirical inquests into human smuggling operations exist. An even smaller number of studies have relied on empirical evidence to understand the structure and enterprise of the groups responsible for the transit of thousands of migrants and refugees worldwide. And despite the role human smuggling has played in making the US–Mexico border one of the most transited borders in the world, the number of studies involving an analysis of the US–Mexico smuggling market is minimal at best (Zhang 2007).

Most of the work on smuggling operations comes from scholars in Europe, who have documented unregulated travel practices into the European Union from countries like Pakistan (Koser 2008), Sri Lanka and Somalia (Van Hear 2004), Afghanistan and Armenia (Bilger et al. 2006; Koser 2009), Albania (Antonopoulus and Winterdyk 2006), the Netherlands (van Liempt 2007; van Liempt and Doomernik 2006) and Turkey (Içduygu and Toktas 2002). Each one of these works has studied human smuggling operations from the perspective of immigrants who were successfully smuggled into their destination countries, providing important understandings of smuggling operations. Yet the voices of those behind the facilitation of immigrants' transits are consistently absent from the discussion. Furthermore, while the above-mentioned studies identify and document the dynamics of the smuggling process, they have mostly been concerned with the financial aspects of the smuggling transaction, paying limited attention to the social interactions that take place or result from that exchange. As Ahmad expresses with disappointment, discussions on smuggling often rely upon one-dimensional portraits of migrant and refugee journeys as solely dictated by economic need (2011, 6–7).

The work of Khalid Koser has been essential in mapping the economic and business aspects of smuggling. His 2008 study on Pakistani immigrants in London described the wide range of financial arrangements that allow for the unrestricted transfer of fees across countries in order to cover immigrants' smuggling costs. Koser found that smuggling is not only profitable for the smuggling facilitators, but also for the customers who hire their services and who, after working for a few years, are able to repay their smuggling fees while supporting themselves in their host countries and contributing to their households' needs in their countries of origin.

In their study of smuggled undocumented immigrants in Austria, scholars like Bilger et al. (2006, 72) identified the importance of taking a closer look at the social interactions between smuggler facilitators and their customers. They have analyzed how facilitators' behaviors are conditioned by customers' perceptions of reliability and trust-worthiness. Bilger and her collaborators refer to smuggling as an "imperfect market" where the degree of competition faced by facilitators forces them to work hard to develop solid reputations to create a sense of trust among clients and potential customers in order to generate business. The study also emphasizes the role finances play in the client/facilitator relationship. Like Koser (2009), Bilger et al. suggest that the quality of smuggling services is ultimately determined by a customer's purchasing power.

This finding was also present in Van Hear's work on Somali and Sri Lankan immigrants (2004). He argues that customers' control of or access to forms of financial capital plays a role in the determination of the routes that are taken by facilitators, the means of transportation used for migration and the destinations reached. Patterns and impacts of migration are shaped by the resources migrants can mobilize, and these resources are in turn dependent on the immigrants' socioeconomic status.

Other analyses of the financial dimension of extralegal border crossings have provided information on the decision-making processes surrounding smuggling journeys (Wheaton et al. 2010); the roles played by the friends and family of migrants in securing or providing resources or other forms of financial assistance (Ahmad 2011; Castro 1998; Içduygu and Toktas 2002; Khosravi 2010); and the terms and conditions governing smuggling agreements (Koser 2008). However, the emphasis in these studies has, once again, been on the financial impact of those who seek to travel, and not that of the smugglers.

Criticisms on the excessive reliance of migration on economic factors refer to their extremely narrow focus on labor factors (see Krissman 2005 in reference to Massey 1999; Massey 1993, 463), yet a way to strengthen these theories of migration has emerged within other forms of inquiry, primarily through studies relying on the inclusion of immigrants' voices and perspectives as sources of knowledge. While much of the discourse of migration continues to often refer to migrants as "anomic loners stuck in cultures of poverty" (Krissman 2005, 8), recent research has noted how immigrant, subaltern and/or highly marginalized groups create, adapt, adopt and develop systems that allow them to improve their lives and those of the people around them within and despite structural limitations. For instance, Rosas (2004) explores the everyday practices of survival among teenagers living within the US–Mexico border sewer system; Gomberg-Muñoz (2010) maps the lives of a group of busboys working at an Italian restaurant in downtown Chicago; while Tellez (2008) describes the quests of immigrant communities to establish political and geographical presences along border towns. Gonzalez-Lopez (2005) shows how Mexican immigrants in the US renegotiate their sexual ideologies and practices and redefine their sexualities, while De Genova's (2005) study on immigrant factory workers in Chicago describes his and his students' attempts to subject state practices to scrutiny and destabilize them. These studies carry intrinsic demands for the re-evaluation of migration scholarship to recognize the abilities and the strengths of migrants. They also enrich the discussion of migration by showing how migrants cultivate their social identities through individual actions.

Agency and migration

The recognition of migrants and refugees as individuals who play a role in their own decision to migrate calls for an analysis of the concept of agency. Agency is understood as an individual's ability to make decisions, even if or when constrained by structural limitations. It also refers to an individual's power to engage in a specific behavior or action that may impact on his or her life in the short or long term. This engagement involves both awareness of the consequences of such behavior or action, and a process through which the individual reflects upon these outcomes. Agency can exist even if subjects' acts are tied and circumscribed to structure, since their actions carry a purposive, instrumental and calculating nature (Emirbayer and Mische 1998) that allows them to exert control in multiple forms.

Conceptualizing agency as inscribed within a structure could convey notions of permanence, consistency and stability (Sewell 1992). Agentic processes, or expressions of agency, however, are dependent on the contextual, temporal conditions of the actors (Emirbayer and Mische 1998; McNay 2003; Sewell 1992), which implies the structures surrounding their actions are prone to change over time. In other words, even in the presence of a structure, individuals can enact multiple behaviors that challenge established norms (as in the case of social movements of resistance and change).

However, much of the work on agency focuses on the durability of structures and not on the way they change over time (McNay 1999, 2003). Despite his impact on theories that emphasize the potential for the transformation of social identities, for example, Foucault's work describes agency largely as a response to repression or constraints. This leads to the definition of agency as a (negative) response to subjection (McNay 2003), reducing the ability of the subject to act upon his or her surroundings.

Agency, however, can also be defined as the multiple ways in which individuals play an *active* role in the *construction* of their lives, despite the negative or constraining nature of structure. By "throwing light on the active processes of self-interpretation [. . .] inherent to the process of subject formation [. . .]," there is the possibility to achieve "an understanding of a creative or imaginative substrate to agency" that can then be "conceptualized to explain how, when faced with complexity and difference, individuals may respond in unexpected and innovative ways that hinder, reinforce or catalyze social change" (McNay 2003, 141).

While Foucault's emphasis on discipline leads to the conception of the body as passive—and therefore dematerializing the experience of agency—Bourdieu incorporates the social *into* the body. For Bourdieu, people are not bound by "unconscious rules" imposed onto them, but are instead able to make choices within the limits imposed by the *habitus* (Nash 2003). Bourdieu also reminds us that social life is a "constant struggle for position, as actors seek (consciously and unconsciously) to weave around the constraints that social structure sets against them" (Dimaggio 1979, 1463). It is the awareness of these very structures on the part of individuals that allows them to act consciously and independently.

The recognition of smuggling as able to embody multiple forms and acts of agency emerges in part from Bourdieu's notion of the habitus and the field, and from his work on the ways the habitus can be embodied, improvised and rein-scribed and/or contradicted (McLeod 2005; McNay 1999). In Foucault's concep-tualization of agency, the lack of a body results in the lack of an active subject through which the agentic process can be carried out (McNay 1999), despite the fact that the body is central to the subject's experience of difference, race, class and gender, and therefore should play a role in any discussion of agency. Bourdieu argues that the social inequalities are established not at the level of the structures (i.e., institutions) but, instead, through the power relations inculcated upon bodies and individuals (Bourdieu 1990, in McNay 1999). It is "the dialectical relation-ship between the body and a socially structured space" that becomes impor-tant, while "embodying the structures of the world" (Bourdieu and Wacquant 1992, 168).

Agency and smuggling

The articulation of multiple forms of agency and the notion of structures as mal-leable allow for individuals' ability to challenge them through time in more than one way, a notion that becomes useful while approaching the study of smuggling. Through agency, migration emerges not only as the result of an economic pres-sure but also as a highly personal, individual process. By considering the role of agency in migration, personal contexts can play even more important roles in an individual's decision to migrate than theories have to date recognized. Migration involves a series of complicated, interconnected circumstances that extend beyond economics—some of which may even challenge our current understandings of power, politics and the economy (Nonini 1997).

Recent studies on smuggling operations seem to incorporate notions of this individual agency in their analyses of population movements. In their study of asylum seekers whose journeys rely on smuggling facilitators, for example, Robinson and Segrott (2002) describe the roles future asylum petitioners play in their interaction with smuggling facilitators, describing it not merely as a finan-cial transaction but instead as a form of collaboration. Would-be asylum seekers engage in long and extremely well-informed decision-making processes in which they consider their individual needs for safety, availability of resources, access to friends and family, etc., even before reaching out to the facilitators who will transport them. In Robinson and Segrott's work, asylum seekers are positioned as the ultimate decision-makers, having the power to decide the course of their lives by staying in their countries and adapting to their local conditions or making the decision to escape the constraints of their country of origin and travel to one where asylum can be sought.

David Spener's work on the strategies used by men of Mexican origin to cross into the US with the assistance of smugglers also identifies how immigrants' decisions to migrate are well-informed and carefully calculated, and take place within the rules and the expectations of the immigrants' community of origin (Spener 2004, 2009b). In other articles, Spener has also challenged some of the most commonly held views of smuggling facilitators as predators or mafia-like (Spener 2004), and has consistently found the networks that facilitate immigrants' transits are instead formed by other immigrants who develop partnerships and rely on network-like collaborations to assist individuals in their personal quests for a new life.

Van Liempt and Doomernik's research on migrants' agency in the smuggling process criticizes Salt and Stein's (1997) model of the smuggling process, which for over a decade dominated most theorizations of the smuggling market. (In Salt and Stein's model, smuggling is described as a primarily economic activity facing little transformation and in which actors play static, limited roles.) Through their interviews with asylum seekers, Van Liempt and Doomernik (2006) identify ways in which immigrants cultivate a relationship with their smuggling facilitators while developing their own protection mechanisms. Their research also found the interactions between immigrants and the people in charge of their transportation are highly complex and not necessarily profit-driven. They identify their respondents' ability to negotiate the terms of their transits as part of smuggling's community-based, non-criminal nature. But given the power differentials that may on occasion exist between smuggling facilitators and their customers, the authors do express concerns over potential abuses being committed during migrants' and refugees' transits.

These studies have contributed to developing a better understanding of the dynamic roles played by both immigrants and the people who facilitate their transits. However, findings have often had a tendency to be restricted to the accounts of the undocumented immigrants or asylum seekers who faced unsuccessful journeys while migrating, and do not come from the men and women who actually facilitated their transits. While migrants are a fundamental source of information into the social dynamics of smuggling in each one of these studies, their knowledge of smuggling operations may be rather limited. Even though many migrants know their facilitators in advance and in contexts different from those related to their migration, their experiences with smugglers are described in these studies as taking place over a very limited span of time—the length of their migratory journeys. This limits our ability to understand some of the social dynamics behind smuggling operations that precede the trans-border journeys. Migrants' experiences with smuggling facilitators are also described primarily as business-like or profit-driven transactions, and provide little insight into the actual dynamics of the smuggling groups.

Several authors have cited safety concerns as the reason behind the absence of the perspectives of smuggling facilitators in their studies. During interviews, some of these scholars have expressed that it is easier to reach out to immigrants than to smuggling facilitators directly. These statements reflect in part the distrust of smugglers on the part of researchers. This fear has played a huge part in the absence of smuggling facilitators' perspectives in analyses of smuggling operations, an absence which has limited our understanding of the activity.

Fortunately, some researchers have managed to overcome these barriers. Perhaps the most comprehensive study regarding human smuggling operations, and the only one to involve extensive contact with smuggling facilitators in the field, is the work of Sheldon Zhang on human smuggling operations from China to the US. Zhang (2008) conducted ethnographic research in the Fuzhou province in China, a renowned snakehead[3] hub and point of departure for thousands of undocumented immigrants bound for the US. As part of his research involving transnational human smuggling, he and his team conducted 129 interviews with men and women involved in the provision of smuggling services. Among his findings, he identified the flexible and highly adaptive nature of smuggling activities, which is at least partially dependent on the community-based nature of the activity. Locals, and not organized crime, are in charge of the recruitment and transportation of migrants. Zhang provides a model of the structure of human smuggling groups that was adopted in and adapted to this project given the striking operational similarities between Chinese and US–Mexico border smuggling facilitators.

Zhang's study was preceded by the work of one of his collaborators, Ko-Lin Chin, who in the late 1990s also conducted research on the activities of snakeheads by interviewing a much smaller group of facilitators within the US detention system (Chin 1999). Joining forces as part of a larger field study on Chinese human smugglers, Zhang and Chin (2002, 2003) concluded that snakeheads are ordinary citizens whose social networks alone provide access to connections and resources to facilitate the transportation of people seeking to leave China. Along with feminist criminologist Jodi Miller, Chin and Zhang have also explored female participation in human smuggling. They found that, while smuggling operations are male-dominated, women play key roles working for or alongside male partners and many times also work on their own to provide services in smuggling operations that involve the least risk of violence or detection (Zhang et al. 2007).

Perhaps one of Zhang's greatest contributions to the study of smuggling operations is his call to uncover the meanings within the everyday interactions among facilitators. He has shown interactions that do not only have an impact on the customer's experience, but also create opportunities allowing for the smuggling facilitator's personal development. In his analysis of women in smuggling operations, for example, he attributes the involvement of large numbers of women in smuggling not to expectations of profit or other potential financial benefits, as other scholars of smuggling would have explained it. Instead, he finds that women have found significant the space they have carved in the market, one where they gain visibility and power and reduce or eliminate any potential stigma surrounding their participation in a criminalized activity.[4]

Each one of these projects has made a fundamental contribution to our understanding of US-bound human smuggling markets, primarily by incorporating the perspectives of human smuggling facilitators, as well as the role played by migrants and refugees, and their families, friends and communities, as agents of mobility. In considering such research, it is vital to understand the smuggling journey as collaborative and involving both the facilitators and those who rely on their services, given that the outcome of a smuggling operation depends greatly upon the collaboration that emerges from these parties' interactions.

Possibilities for exploring the smuggling market beyond a single geographic context, its financial dimensions or national security implications have emerged from a critical body of work that investigates the role of the state in deliberately creating conditions of risk at global frontiers which directly impact the security of irregular border crossers (Pickering 2011; Weber and Pickering 2011). In this context, risk does not merely refer to the disciplining and criminalization of irregular forms of mobility, but also to the ways in which specific border control policies and practices, whether intentionally or unintentionally, impact human lives.

Increased awareness about the global criminalization of migration and the role played by border enforcement in generating risk and harm has challenged social scientists to engage more in interdisciplinary research (Pickering and McCulloch 2012). Pickering and Weber's extensive body of work on globalization and borders has provided evidence of how the enforcement of border control policies is the primary cause of death along global frontiers. Their work relies on the testimonies of hundreds of illegalized border crossers, which demonstrates how "the ever expanding matrix of deterrence and risk is constantly being built and rebuilt by the complex interplay between official policy, migrant motivation and opportunities for criminal enterprise" (Weber and Pickering 2011, 7). Echoing Andreas and Greenhill (2010), Pickering and Weber criticize the emphasis placed on quantification, which has had the effect of normalizing the multiple forms of violence against border crossers worldwide. They call instead for researchers, policy makers and others to *account* for deaths resulting from structural and interpersonal violence.

Building on their work, the current project seeks to identify the role of state-sponsored forms of border policing and control in shaping the emergence and consolidation of smuggling services, and the implications in the lives of extralegal border crossers along the US–Mexico border. Simultaneously, it explores the apparent contradictions and challenges inherent to smuggling (such as the human smuggler's role in facilitating a safe transit while also having to rely on travel via increasingly dangerous routes; the perception of smuggling as protective despite its potential violence; and its collaborative, community-based nature against the high fees involved).

In sum, this book contributes to the collective, interdisciplinary efforts of scholars seeking to map the mechanisms that criminalize and punish human mobility along the global frontier, as well as their implications (see Pickering and McCulloch 2012; Pickering 2011; Weber and Pickering 2011). It also examines smuggling as an everyday social practice performed along the contemporary deterritorialized global borders, where smuggling facilitators, their clients and the communities to which they belong work—even if disjointedly—at circumventing the limitations imposed on human mobility by the nation-state. It does so by emphasizing the ways in which human smugglers and border crossers seek to legitimize, justify and protect their activities and identities, and to maintain a sense of dignity in the context of the militarization and enforcement of the border in the US state of Arizona.

Smuggling the world in

As early as 2001, characterizations of human smuggling facilitators as greedy rapists, kidnappers and extortionists, gang members and even as transplants of Mexican drug cartels were common in the rhetoric of Arizona's local media and politicians. Smuggling facilitators came to be described as possessing a natural inclination to hurt their clients, taking their meager earnings and abandoning them to die in the unforgiving Arizona desert. Media rhetoric further established – primarily through the most graphic of cases—notions of human smugglers as operating as highly coordinated, well-oiled machines responding to a centralized command, and whose leaders did not think twice about using violence to crush rivals or "conquer" new "territories." Furthermore, the emphasis on the transnational nature of smuggling through the use of references like "south of the border" revealed a concern over the spread of transnational crime, the racial undertones shaping the discussions over irregular migration.

Yet Arizona's human smuggling facilitators have not been alone in this characterization. Globally, whether it be Australia, the Middle East, the Mediterranean coasts or the frigid waters of Canada, those behind irregular transits are time and again described as members of large, structured, hierarchical, violent, territorial, profit-driven, transnational criminal networks comprising men of color operating in the shadows. Said narratives are frequently accompanied by statements describing smuggling groups as having unlimited resources at their disposal, their tentacles expanding beyond the borders of a specific country, raking in millions, sometimes billions, of dollars in profits. And yet, most criminal investigations result only in the arrest of a few of the so-called organized, professional criminals, if any at all (in fact, the majority of smuggling arrests involve irregular migrants in transit, rather than their smugglers) (Ahmad 2011; Eagly 2011). And while significant emphasis is given to highlight profits and finances, most of those involved belong to the working class, are often employed and lack criminal backgrounds. And as far as transnational connections go, most smuggling-related activities occur at the local level, and only involve local facilitators.

As in the case of other highly politicized phenomena like terrorism, drug trafficking or weapons smuggling, the constant repetition of sensationalistic facts often accompanied by an overreliance on numerical projections—or, as Peter Andreas calls it, a preoccupation with quantification and data (Andreas and Greenhill 2010)—has facilitated the circulation and engraining of distorted notions surrounding smuggling. The emphasis on smuggling as a crime has often been connected to the mobility of those living in the global south, allowing for the practices related to human mobility to be perceived not as humanitarian crises, but as pressing national security issues afflicting the industrialized north. This is despite the fact that the number of international migrants and refugees worldwide constitute only about 3 percent of the world's entire population and that most migratory movements take place within developing countries, and most refugees remain within the global south (IOM 2013; UNHCR 2013). Yet the numbers cited in connection to migration have been used to develop a rhetoric that denotes most forms of mobility as irregular. And in so doing, migration tends to be construed as an invasion of unprecedented magnitude, threatening the contemporary nation-state, justifying the implementation of intensified controls and regulations, leading to the emergence of new forms of criminalization.

Within the rhetoric of a global north at siege, threatened by the arrival of foreigners, refugees and migrants, human smuggling facilitators emerge as global criminals operating in the shadows, eager to overcome nations' efforts at securing their borders. Official accounts of human smuggling continue to be those explaining the scope and nature of smuggling within typical narratives of gangs, mafias and ethnic syndicates, or defining smugglers' actions along narratives of victimization, sexual violence or financial exploitation. The questions pertaining to the social organization of smuggling and its day-to-day practices thus remain unanswered. Are smugglers responsible for all forms of irregular migration? Are all forms of smuggling violent or predatory? Is there a social basis for smuggling? What are the motivations behind a career in smuggling, if such—as argued by law enforcement—exists? How do smuggling facilitators respond or adapt to increased levels of surveillance and control? The following chapters draw from the testimonies of smuggling facilitators and those who rely on their services along one of the most transited borders in the world in order to answer these questions.

Notes

1 For a sample of journalistic coverage on smuggling, see Galindo (2014) "Police: Human smuggler jailed after raping immigrant twice"; Grado (2014) "Prosecutor wants executions for human smugglers"; Pavlich (2013) "Human smuggling picking up steam in Southern Arizona"; Tietz (2012) "The US–Mexico border's 150 miles of hell."
2 For example, the American and the Australian governments have launched extensive campaigns in migrant-generating countries aimed at creating fear and distrust of smugglers among those considering traveling extralegally. The impact of these campaigns at deterring extralegal border crossings, however, is difficult if not impossible to determine.
3 Folk name given to Chinese human smuggling facilitators.
4 "In a business full of uncertainties and hazards, when gendered cultural expectations are compared with a successful reputation, a female snakehead can command significant respect" (Zhang 2008, 205).

2 Coyotes in the era of enforcement

The emergence of Arizona's human smuggling market and the criminalization of migration

> We cannot afford all this illegal immigration and everything that comes with it, everything from the crime and to the drugs and the kidnappings and the extortion and the beheadings and the fact that people can't feel safe in their community. It's wrong! It's wrong!
>
> (Jane Brewer, Arizona's governor)

On the morning of April 23, 2010, journalists from around the world descended upon Phoenix, Arizona, to witness the signing of the *Support Our Law Enforcement and Safe Neighborhoods Act*, infamously known as SB1070, signed by Jane Brewer, Arizona's governor, who had—as the quote above states—made her distaste over the presence of irregular migrants clear. Among its main provisions, SB1070 grants local law enforcement officers the authority to determine the immigration status of someone arrested or detained when there is "reasonable suspicion" he or she is not in the US legally (State of Arizona 2010).

SB1070 was introduced in the Arizona Congress by local politicians who had openly expressed their distaste toward the presence of Latino residents in the state (Robbins 2008), which in turn raised immediate concerns over the law's potential implications for race relations. There was in fact widespread unease about the likelihood of SB1070 being used by law enforcement to justify and conduct stops and arrests against minorities (Valle del Sol et al. v. Michael B. Whiting et al., CV10-01061-PHX-SRB), as well as concerns over the long-term impact of the law in a community already marked by a history of racial discrimination and prejudice. Some local law enforcement agencies conveyed their distress over the impact the law would have on police–community relations and on the potential for increased vulnerability and victimization among irregular migrants who might decide not to report a crime committed against them, fearing arrest (US Department of Justice 2012). There were also reports of large numbers of residents of Latino origin leaving the state in anticipation of the law's signing, fearing further acts of racism, discrimination and intimidation (Cohn 2012). In summary, the introduction of SB1070 set in motion a wide range of reactions, which eventually helped to propel its visibility, as well as that of the state of Arizona—one of four US states on the border with Mexico, and commonly referred to as "ground zero" of the American debate over irregular migration.

Since its inception, SB1070 was consistently described as unprecedented; and as one of the most, if not the most, controversial pieces of immigration control in America's contemporary history (NALEO 2012; Santos 2012). Yet the portrayal of the law as extraordinary or unparalleled obscured the long list of legislative measures that throughout US history have been used to justify the removal of populations deemed as unwanted or which have perpetuated the structural conditions that allow for their discrimination, primarily on the basis of race and class. In this context, SB1070 was in fact only one among hundreds of pieces of legislation that, during the first decade of the twenty-first century, were approved by legislatures throughout the US with a very specific purpose: to criminalize the presence of immigrants of color in the country (Gordon and Raja 2012).[1] Furthermore, the characterization of SB1070 as unique masked the long history of Arizonan legislation and enforcement practices targeting the presence of non-Anglo residents in the state.

This chapter examines the socio-economic and historical contexts that have shaped race relations in Arizona, with specific reference to border crossings and migration. It argues that, contrary to official narratives that designate the presence of migrants in the state as a contemporary problem or crisis, Arizona has historically struggled with the presence of minority residents, the state having intentionally engaged in the creation of structural conditions that facilitate their marginalization, discrimination and segregation. In contrast with a significant portion of the contemporary scholarship on border control, which has focused primarily on the impact of current legislation on migrants' legal or civil rights (Romero 2006), I take a historical approach to demonstrate that the conditions that allowed for the passage of laws aimed at criminalizing migration in Arizona by the turn of the twenty-first century are part of a multi-level, multi-actor continuum of initiatives aimed at maintaining racial inequality and enforcing immigration flows in that state. While recognizing that many other ethnic groups have faced discriminatory acts and violence at the hands of the state, I focus on the experiences of Latinos, given their role as one of the state's largest minority groups and their hyper-representation as dangerous and criminal in the dominant discourse and initiatives on immigration, national security and border control.

A second goal of this chapter is to trace how Arizona's historical efforts to control the Latino presence in the state coalesced with those of the federal government aimed at criminalizing irregular migration, particularly in the context of the emergence of Maricopa County as the country's major hub for human smuggling operations. Of central importance was the implementation of federal border control policies in the 1990s, which rerouted the flow of irregular migration from the more used routes of Texas and California into the Arizona desert and created the conditions for increased vulnerability and risk among those seeking to cross the border extralegally, leading to exponential increases in the numbers of deaths (Whiteford et al. 2013; Rubio-Goldsmith et al. 2006).

Lastly, and once the structural conditions that allowed for the development of the market are examined, the chapter discusses SB1372—the Coyote Law—as an example of how popular characterizations of the human smuggler as violent and predatory were used to target and criminalize extralegal border crossers in Arizona. While initially articulated as a mechanism to protect migrants from the abuses of human smugglers, SB1372 was, until late 2013, used to charge extralegal border crossers (the overwhelming majority of whom are irregular migrants of Latino origin) with conspiring to commit their own human smuggling. The measure did not merely lead to the conviction of thousands of people. I will argue that, eventually, it altered the social fabric that once allowed for the safe provision of border crossing services by smuggling facilitators who, concerned over the outcome of enforcement, changed their tactics by increasingly recruiting migrants as facilitators, ultimately reducing the safety of those seeking to cross the border extralegally and increasing their likelihood of arrest.

The Mexican presence in Arizona

The majority of non-white residents in the state of Arizona are individuals of Mexican origin. This is explained in great measure by Arizona's geographic proximity to Mexico. The Mexican presence in Arizona can indeed be traced back many generations, given the state's past as Mexican territory (Benton-Cohen 2004; Meeks 2006; Officer 1987; Oberle and Arreola 2008). The land that now constitutes Arizona was acquired from the Mexican government as part of the agreements known as the Gagdsen Purchase, which were signed in 1853. Despite the change of ownership, whole sections of Arizona—particularly those closest to the Mexican border—retained their traditional Sonoran character, with people from both countries maintaining rich social, economic and political connections (McConnell 2013, 3).

The first white residents—referred locally as Anglos—arrived later in the nineteenth century, attracted by the booming mining industry. New migrants from Germany, Ireland and England married local residents, established businesses and adopted the Southwest's farming and ranching methods (Oberle and Arreola 2008, 4; Benton-Cohen and Cadava 2010, 5). Border crossings—today the subject of continued debates over national security and immigration—were hardly discussed in relation to regulation or control. People on both sides of the largely unpatrolled divide would cross it at will (Benton-Cohen and Cadava 2010, 6–7). In fact it was not until 1918 that the federal government started to keep track of crossings, and it would take another six years for the US Border Patrol to be founded.

While the intensity of commerce and the apparent freedom of mobility gave the impression of a well-integrated society, racial tensions marked the everyday lives of the state's residents. In fact by the end of the nineteenth century racism and discrimination had already created the foundation of the structures that would prevent Mexican migrants and families residing in Arizona from exercising social, political and economic mobility (the Gagdsen Purchase alone, for example, granted US citizenship to the Mexican nationals who lived in the newly acquired territory, yet denied them the right to participate in political office) (Gómez 2007).

Interracial conflict has been an ongoing occurrence in the state, with multiple events having helped maintain and reinforce the subordinated status of

Mexican-Americans and incoming migrants of Mexican origin to the state—most of whom were working class citizens (Romero 2006). From the onset, residents of Mexican origin were commonly referred to as less than human, inherently criminal, and prone to poverty and disease.

Immigration and border policy

While the list is long, there are a few central events that had substantial impact in creating the structures that over time have maintained racial inequality in the state, to wit: the race-based, two-tier wage system; state-sanctioned labor laws that restricted occupations by race; redlining and housing allocations and settlement ordinances; and the chilling effect created by the legal repercussions of anti-immigrant enforcement practices (including events like the Hanigan incident in 1976 and the Chandler Roundup in 1997).

Characterized by sociologists and historians of labor as one of the most defining moments in the construction of structural inequality in Arizona, the two-tier labor system implemented in Arizona's mines established a compensation system based on by race, with Mexican laborers (who constituted the majority of those working in the mines) being paid half the salaries of Anglo workers despite performing identical tasks; furthermore, occupations were determined on the basis of race, and workers of Mexican origin were not allowed to move into higher-paying categories, which were reserved for Anglo workers (Benton-Cohen and Cadava 2010, 7). In addition, labor unions frequently engaged in discriminatory actions as part of their efforts to advance the interests of their majority members, who were Anglo. As early as 1910, white labor coalitions tried to set limits on the number of immigrant workers hired, concerned over the presence of workers of Mexican origin at the mines. By 1914, an initiative mandating that four out of every five employees in any workplace be American citizens was approved by public vote. While the law referred to non-American citizens, citizenship was racially based; and so while Anglo and European workers were protected by the law, workers of Mexican origin continued to be perceived as foreigners regardless of their citizenship status (Benton-Cohen and Cadava 2010, 8).

Over time, labor unions reticently began to acknowledge the potential political power of Mexican workers and opted to incorporate them into some of their attempts at improving working conditions at the mines. Some of these efforts backfired. The endeavors of labor unions in the town of Bisbee in 1917 to eliminate the race-based dual wage system were immediately misconstrued by Anglo residents and mine owners as evidence of Mexican residents' "hostility," and rumors began to circulate that unionized mine workers were planning an uprising. Cochise County Sheriff Harry Wheeler, supported by prominent mine managers and a large posse of deputies, arrested hundreds of residents believed to be foreign in the mining town of Bisbee, forcefully removing them from their homes and businesses, placing them in boxcars and expelling them from Arizona. The event primarily impacted families of Mexican origin, who constituted the majority of those living in the mining camps. People were afraid or suspicious of their neighbors. Many families lost their main source of income; some opted to abandon their homes rather than endure further mistreatment and humiliation, and most of the "deported" workers never returned (Benton-Cohen 2004; Benton-Cohen and Cadava 2010, 11; Watson 1977).

Acts of intimidation and violence against non-Anglo residents continued to take place in Arizona in the decades that followed, most commonly during times of economic distress. Mass deportations involving Mexican and Mexican-American workers were frequent in the 1930s as the once powerful mining industry and thriving cotton trade were hit during the Great Depression. In 1931, Arizona's Board of Public Welfare justified cuts to services and allowances for Mexican-American families claiming that they had lower standards of living than those of their Anglo counterparts (Leighninger 2003, 86). The allowances for Anglo families, however, were significantly increased.

By the end of WWII, the labor system had allowed for Arizona's racialized class structure to remain virtually intact. The state's economy continued to depend on the availability of low-paid labor provided primarily by Mexican-Americans, Native Americans and African-Americans working the farm fields. The introduction of the Bracero Program (a temporary labor initiative aimed at reducing the impact of the labor shortage caused by the war, which relied on the importation of laborers from Mexico) further reinforced the perception of farm work as the "quintessential form of Mexican labor" (Meeks 2006, 92).

While the boom of Arizona's urban centers in the late 1940s and early 1950s yielded some improvements in the economic status of Mexican and Mexican-American residents in the state through the lessening of some of the race-based employment restrictions, a new concern over the presence of people of Mexican origin emerged. Allegations over the spread of irregular migration as a result of the Bracero Program (and claims that thousands of Mexican workers had overstayed in the country illegally) led to the US Border Patrol engaging in a series of immigration raids in agricultural areas of the state (Hernandez 2010). The massive nature of these raids created the illusion that the "immigration crisis" had to be solved—Operation Wetback, which targeted farm workers from the agricultural fields in Eastern California and Western Arizona, yielded 11,000 arrests during its first week alone (Koestler 2010).

The economic downturn of the 1970s marked the start of another period of racial tension in Arizona. Decreasing oil supplies and a slowdown of the cattle and mining industries hindered the state's economy. In Arizona, the downturn was once again blamed on Mexican workers, who were perceived as taking jobs away from "legitimate" residents. This time around, however, as Cadava (2010) points out, civil rights organizations began to express concern over instances of violence against Mexican-Americans and Mexicans along the US–Mexico border, including torture and murders at the hands of law enforcement officials.

It was under this heightened state of attention that Arizona found itself at the center of a binational controversy. On August 18, 1976, three young Mexican men reported to the Mexican authorities having been robbed and tortured by two Arizona ranchers, the Hanigan brothers, as they walked through their property in an attempt to enter the US extralegally. The Hanigans first questioned and then robbed the men, holding them against their will and "[hanging] them from a tree; burning their feet, and holding a knife to their genitals before firing more than 100 rounds of birdshot into their backs" (Cadava 2010, 15).

The district attorney filed criminal charges against the Hanigans and the case went to trial. The court found the defendants not guilty when the state ruled that the victims, by virtue of being "illegal aliens," were not entitled to civil rights protections. Given the victims' immigration status (all three had crossed the border irregularly), the court determined no crime could have taken place, and therefore the accused could not be charged (Cadava 2010, 16). A second trial resulted in a mistrial.

The Hanigans had the support of a large segment of the state's population, who were frustrated by what was characterized as the inaction of the federal government to secure the border. Immigrant advocates, civil rights organizations and government officials in both the US and Mexico used the case to condemn the violent acts systematically committed against individuals of Mexican origin in the US. Under pressure, the US Government eventually filed federal charges against the ranchers. A third trial found Patrick Hanigan guilty, while his brother was once again acquitted of all charges. The Hanigans' father, who was also initially charged, had died by the end of the six-year legal process.

The effect of federal immigration policy: IRCA, Gatekeeper and Hold the Line

In the years that followed the Hanigan incident, race relations in Arizona continued to be tense amid the growing anxiety nationwide over the presence of irregular Mexican migrants in the US. Calls to the US Congress to address what was characterized as a crisis of illegal immigration had been made since the early 1970s, but it was not until 1986 that the Immigration Reform and Control Act (IRCA) was approved. The IRCA was the most comprehensive amnesty reform of the twentieth century, on the one hand regularizing the status of all individuals who had entered the country without authorization prior to 1982, while on the other, establishing strong sanctions against employers who hired undocumented migrants, and calling for increased border enforcement levels along the US–Mexico divide.

The architects of the law believed that increased enforcement would serve as a deterrent to those seeking to enter the US extralegally, and that the punishments associated with illegal hiring practices would reduce the appeal of employing undocumented workers (Cornelius 2001, 695). Indeed, there was a considerable drop in the number of arrests conducted by the Immigration and Naturalization Service immediately following the passage of the act—a reduction that at least initially was interpreted as an indicator of its success.

And yet, only a few years following the enactment of the law, irregular migration had returned to pre-IRCA levels. In fact, scholars have argued that the legalization paths opened by the IRCA propelled the migration of considerable numbers of Mexican and other nationals from Latin America who had until then not considered seeking work in the US, but who, as a result of the migration of their friends and relatives, became aware of the mechanisms that would allow for their legalization (Cornelius 1989, 697). By the early 1990s, the increased visibility of Mexican and Central American irregular migrants (whose migration was also deeply intertwined with the US military-sponsored conflicts that afflicted those nations during most of the 1980s) began to raise questions over the effectiveness of the IRCA and its provisions, particularly in migrant destination states like California and Texas.

Fueled by political and polemical statements from local politicians and immigration officials on the dangers of irregular migration, and intensive media coverage characterizing migrants as crime and violence prone, the collective hysteria over the presence of Latino migrants along the border escalated (Nevins 2010, 97). A slowdown in the economy, as well as political pressure that mobilized concerns over the presence of Latinos, did not however force Washington to pay attention to the renewed demands for immigration and border control.

In September 1993, Operation Blockade (later renamed Hold the Line) was singlehandedly implemented by Silvestre Reyes, the Border Patrol Chief of the El Paso Sector in Texas, who without giving notice to Washington deployed 400 agents and their vehicles along a 20-mile stretch of the border between Texas and Mexico, in what marked a radical departure from the former strategy of pursuing and apprehending irregular migrants once they had crossed the border. As a result of the new approach, extralegal border crossings in the region decreased dramatically—if only temporarily (Nevins 2010, 111). Reyes's actions and their outcomes were applauded, further increasing the pressure on the administration of President Bill Clinton to devise a new border control strategy aimed at deterring unauthorized crossings.

Following Reyes's albeit temporary success, politicians in California called for the adoption of a similar strategy in their state. Following hasty negotiations and heavy political campaigning in the media, on October 1, 1994, Operation Gatekeeper was launched along the Californian border with Mexico. It involved the deployment of large numbers of Border Patrol officers and surveillance resources across the San Diego Border Patrol district (which had the highest incidence of extralegal border crossings in the country). By following a strategy similar to that adopted by Reyes, Gatekeeper was also effective at decreasing apprehension numbers and reducing the number of extralegal crossings (Nevins 2010).

One of the most important and lasting implications of both strategies involved the shifting of the flow of extralegal border crossers east of California into the Arizona desert, in the belief that the desert's environmental conditions would serve as a strong deterrent to those seeking to cross the border irregularly and reduce the likelihood of crossings into Texas and California (Cornelius 2001).

It is undeniable that Gatekeeper and Hold the Line were ultimately effective at reducing extralegal border crossings in their respective border districts. Their enforcement resulted in the redirection of irregular border crossers into more isolated sections of the border—specifically, the Arizona desert—where the US

Border Patrol believed that arrests would be easier to handle. However, a troubling indicator of the impact of both operations began to unravel not too long thereafter. As numerous scholars have pointed out, the forcing of the border crossers into the less-explored routes of the Arizona desert not only reduced arrests on once overran border crossing points; the shift eventually led to an increase in the number of deaths of irregular border crossers, as they were driven into riskier and more remote areas of the desert in order to avoid detection, becoming exposed to the extreme desert environment, a trend which has continued to this day (Rubio-Goldsmith et al. 2006; Cornelius 1989; Massey et al. 2003; Martinez et al. 2013). While the deaths have been characterized as "an unintended consequence" of US federal border control strategies (Ermolaeva and Ross 2010; Nuñez-Neto and Vina 2005; Stellar and Ibarra 2002) it is impossible to believe that in the context of an operation of this magnitude they were not widely anticipated (Magana 2008).

The emergence of the Arizona human smuggling market

According to US Border Patrol statistics, prior to the introduction of Gatekeeper and Hold the Line, most people seeking to cross the border extralegally had opted for the traditional corridors into California and Texas. Arizona, home to the inhospitable Sonoran Desert, had not been a site of intense border crossing activity. In fact, in the years that preceded the implementation of Hold the Line and Gatekeeper, only about 15 percent of all Border Patrol apprehensions occurred in the Tucson District. But by 1999 the same district had become the single most traversed corridor for irregular border crossers along the entire US–Mexico border (US Border Patrol 2013, quoted in Martinez et al. 2013, 11).

The impact of enforcement along this section of the border has indeed been demonstrated quantitatively via the increase in the number of apprehensions, but also in the number of recovered human remains. Over the decade that followed the border control initiative, the Tucson sector of the US Border Patrol reported the highest number of human casualties (Martinez et al. 2013). The relevance of the correlation between enforcement and lethality became even clearer when, by the turn of the first decade of the twenty-first century, researchers identified that the number of deaths had increased despite the record low number of arrests (Whiteford et al. 2013).[2]

While the tragic dimensions of the humanitarian crisis arising from failed federal border control policy must not be forgotten, one of the lesser explored implications has been Arizona's emergence as the main point of extralegal border crossings into the US. By displacing the flow of irregular border crossers into more remote areas of the desert, law enforcement did not merely create new migration corridors; it also created the demand for border crossing services along a new segment to the border: the Arizona–Sonora region.

The provision of extralegal border crossing services has been a constant part of the US–Mexico border subterranean economy, enabling people to cross the border without documents for most of the twentieth century. Gamio documented, through interviews in the late 1920s, how irregular migrants seeking to enter the

US through Arizona recalled being transported by individual facilitators who worked on their own or in small groups of two or three facilitators:

> The smugglers, or "coyotes," who manage the illegal crossing of the immi-grants work as individuals and also in gangs. These people know their ground thoroughly, and the habits of both American and Mexican authorities, and sometimes they even have an arrangement with some district official; there-fore they are generally successful in taking their human cargo over. They charge as a rule from five to ten dollars a piece, and more if there is baggage or in unusual cases. [. . .] when the smugglers form a gang, they have men on both sides, either in the offices or along the banks of the river—depending on their system—and they employ a set of signals to avoid an armed clash with the authorities, which nevertheless sometimes occurs.
>
> (Gamio 1930, 205–206)

By the late 1990s, Arizona was on track to become the country's top border cross-ing point, if the number of Border Patrol arrests is used as an indicator. For dec-ades, immigration-related arrest numbers in Arizona were among the lowest in the country, its border terrain and extreme climate making it an unlikely route. Furthermore, despite its proximity to Mexico, the state was not a migrant des-tination of the kind of California, Texas or Illinois, where large Mexican and increasingly Central American diasporas were well incorporated into the urban economies. While acts like the Hanigan incident attest to the presence of undocu-mented migrants in Arizona—and Arizonans' distaste over their presence—the state had primarily been a transit destination for migrants en route to other cities within the United States.

By the late 1990s, the demand for guides who could assist migrants with their border crossings had already moved to the Arizona border. Enforcement had indeed been effective at limiting border crossings along specific segments of the US–Mexico border. But along the Arizona/Sonora border, it also resulted in the emergence of local groups and households of individuals who, relying on their own resources, began to provide services to assist those seeking to cross the bor-der extralegally (Rochkind 2009). The closing or suspension of the traditional border crossing routes due to increased enforcement did not stop migration flows. It simply translated into the demand for smuggling services.

By the late 1990s, small communities in the proximity of the Mexican side of the border with Arizona, like those of Naco, Agua Prieta and Altar, began to witness an influx of people looking for assistance with their border crossings (Trevizo 2013). Historically impoverished and marginalized, and facing few employment options, members of these communities started to provide border crossing assistance to the growing number of people traveling to this section of the border hoping to cross into the US. These towns gradually earned a reputation as locations from where border crossing assistance or guidance could be obtained (Harman 2006). Local residents in turn relied on their proximity to Arizona and their access to vast social networks within the state to start offering full-service border crossings.

It appears the growth of the human smuggling market was therefore a result of the increased demand to facilitate specific segments of particular border crossing transits for arriving migrants—opportunities shared among border residents and their friends and families—amid increased enforcement. Facilitated by traditions of extended household and community-based efforts to overcome sudden periods of unemployment or other forms of economic difficulty, participation in smuggling facilitation thus became one of the few opportunities available to men and women along the US–Mexico border, disenfranchised by virtue of marginalization, immigration, race or employment status, to generate an income, even if supplemental.

While Gatekeeper and Hold the Line had devastating humanitarian consequences, as evidenced in the number of deaths and the reports of violence targeting migrants in transit, they also had a significant, if often neglected, consequence. They ultimately fueled the development of the local human smuggling market. By 2003, federal agencies had begun to acknowledge Arizona's role in the US human smuggling market (Torres 2004), and by 2005 the state had been designated as the main point of entry for undocumented migration into the US (Los Angeles Times 2010), primarily on the basis of Border Patrol arrest numbers and smuggling-related incidents in the cities and towns along I-10, the interstate highway connecting the border to the state's interior.

Maricopa County

By 2003, the metropolitan area of Maricopa County had become the thirteenth largest metropolitan area in the US; its growth had placed it among the 10 most rapidly expanding economies in the country (Lara-Valencia and Fisher 2013). Efforts to attract high-tech and pharmaceutical companies to the region had paid off, with high-wage occupations becoming abundant and housing demand growing at record speeds. Located along the interstate highway 10, one of the major transportation corridors in North America, the region was also on its way to becoming one of the most important technological hubs in the country, which would allow Arizona to shift from a resource-based production economy to a technologically driven one (Lara-Valencia and Fisher 2013, 129).

Despite its technological and economic progress, Maricopa County was also one of the most racially segregated jurisdictions in the country, as a result of extensive redlining and segregationist efforts which had, since the 1880s, confined residents of Mexican origin to the least-desirable part of the region. Arizonans of Mexican origin were restricted to settling in the outskirts of what today constitutes Downtown Phoenix, along the flood-prone banks of the Salt River, and in proximity to the agricultural fields where they worked (Lukinbeal et al. 2010). These sections of the metropolitan area became stigmatized as the Mexican neighborhoods, becoming endemically afflicted by poverty and lack of services. Today, these sections continue to be occupied primarily by working class residents of Mexican origin, a constant reminder of decades of segregation (Bolin et al. 2005). These communities are also in the part of the county where acts of vigilantism and hyper-policing by local and federal law enforcement agencies targeting migrants have occurred with most frequency.

Acts to limit the social, economic and political participation of ethnic minorities are not limited to geographic settlements. In 2006 alone, the Arizona Legislature approved 37 immigration-related bills (O'Leary and Sanchez 2011, 119). Legislation like the *Legal Arizona Workers' Act* established penalties against employers who knowingly hired "unauthorized aliens," even though the law was only ever used against employees rather than employers and has never resulted in criminal charges being filed against any business owner (Valle del Sol et al. v. Goddard, 2007; Carlton 2010). The *Arizona Taxpayer and Citizens Protection Act* required voters to show proof of citizenship in order to register to vote. Proposition 300 restricted eligibility for state-funded educational services to those who could provide proof of legal residence. Proposition 100 denied the right to bail to individuals who could not provide evidence of their legal immigration status. In multiple jurisdictions, the enforcement of these initiatives involved acts of intimidation and hyper-vigilance against those residing in predominantly immigrant communities throughout the state. Arrests were frequently televised, with images of police officers handcuffing disheveled detainees, who were primarily people of color arrested on their way to work, at their places of employment or while driving their children to school or church.

Perhaps the most infamous of all Arizona's statutes was the *Support our Safe Neighborhoods and Law Enforcement Act*, known widely as SB1070. From its inception, SB1070's language was clear in expressing its creators' animosity toward residents of Latino origin in the state, who were consistently described as Arizona's quasi-criminal element (Provine and Sanchez 2011). Latino migrants continue to be blamed for a wide range of socio-economic problems afflicting the state—among them, the perceived increase in the number of irregular migrants in Arizona. While the clear racial undertones of SB1070 put it at the front and center of the US immigration debate, there were other pieces of approved legislation of a profiling nature which had serious legal repercussions on the lives of Arizona's Latino residents.

At the same time that the constitutionality of SB1070 was being debated in court and in the public domain, a statute relying on racial profiling for its execution was already allowing for the conviction of hundreds of extralegal border crossers: SB1372, known informally as the Coyote Law.

The creation of a crisis: the anti-human smuggling statute in Arizona

> I reached the drivers [sic] window. He stepped out and I had him lay on the ground. I looked to my rear and I saw that the occupants of the window van were getting out. *They were all getting out and sitting on the ground next to it.* It appeared to me that more then [sic] 20 people exited the van. I then walked to the second van and again found more then [sic] 20 people had gotten out of it. Once I got all the passengers together I counted them and determined that I had 53 possibly illegal aliens in my custody. I instructed all of them to sit on the ground and to stay seated. At 10:17 the first MCSO units arrived. We started interviews at 11:30.
>
> (Burke, G.A., 2006)

In the early hours of March 2, 2006, George Burke, an officer from the Maricopa County Sheriff's Office, was getting ready to wrap up his shift. Overnight he had been patrolling a largely uninhabited section of the county known as Harquahala Valley, located along a remote desert road used mostly by local farmers and utility workers. Burke had in fact just radioed in to let the dispatcher know that he was heading back to the station when something unusual caught his attention. According to his report, Burke noticed two vehicles heading in his direction that suddenly stopped and turned around before heading back into the desert trail. Initially Burke believed that the vehicles "might be the power company coming to do some kind of work." But as he approached them, he noticed that one "had Sonara [sic] Mexico plates" (Burke 2006).

Burke made no reference to the plates during his in-court testimony, when instead he claimed that it had been his "training and experience" working in Maricopa County—"a well-known smuggling corridor"—that told him "something was going on" (Billeaud 2006).

Burke's report goes on to describe how the first vehicle pulled to the side of the road upon his command. He approached the driver's side and, without having questioned the driver, Burke noticed three other people sitting in the front seat area. At this point, suspecting that he was dealing with a case of human smuggling, the officer pulled out his weapon and ordered the driver to step out of the vehicle.

As the driver lay on the ground, Burke heard the back door of the van open. He witnessed a group of approximately 20 people step out of the vehicle in silence, sitting by the side of the desert road. Burke had not even had a chance to call for assistance when he noticed a second group of people of approximately the same size walking in his direction, having stepped out of the *second* vehicle and quietly joining the first group. It was not until then that Burke called for support. It took at least an hour and a half for backup to arrive, and another hour or so before bilingual officers could be dispatched to the remote Harquahala Valley to interview the men and women identified as extralegal border crossers. By the end of the morning, 54 Mexican nationals between the ages of 18 and 46 had been placed under arrest for entering the US extralegally. The driver of the first vehicle was expected to be charged with facilitating the group's illegal entry. All 54 detainees were transported to the Maricopa County jail, where they were initially processed for deportation and removal proceedings later that day. Yet that same afternoon, in a dramatic turn of events, Andrew Thomas, then Maricopa County's prosecutor, announced all 54 detainees would be charged under the terms of the Coyote Law as having co-conspired to commit their own human smuggling (Kiefer 2006).

A relatively new piece of legislation, SB1372 had been implemented in an attempt to impose sanctions against the coyotes who preyed upon migrants and border crossers in transit. According to Thomas's statements, however, the statute allowed for the state to file charges not only against smugglers, but also against those who collaborated with them to facilitate their own transits. Under this rationale, the 54 border crossers arrested by Burke had committed an act of conspiracy to commit smuggling by establishing an agreement with the smuggler (MCAO 2005).

Thomas's interpretation of the statute generated an almost immediate reaction on the part of immigrant advocates and concerned legal experts. Legal teams nationwide were assembled in order to articulate a response to the charges (as in the case of the We are America/Somos America Coalition[3]), and the Mexican Secretary of State retained legal representation for its citizens, since the majority of those arrested were of Mexican origin (La Jeunesse 2006). All initial court challenges were, however, fruitless.

After months of court hearings, the men and women detained at Harquahala, homesick and worn out by the length of the legal process, started to accept plea agreements for conspiracy charges as a way out of detention. Under the pleas' terms, those detained were granted probation on the condition that they did not return to the US illegally. Their acceptance of the pleas, however, eliminated the possibility of these cases prosecuted under the Coyote Law of being ever formally reviewed or challenged in court (Eagly 2011, 1754). By early July, of the 51 people indicted, 28 had pleaded guilty following their plea offer and were sentenced to probation terms of varied lengths and deported.

Despite counting on the initial support of Arizona's court system, Thomas's office was also fully aware of the unlikelihood that the conspiracy argument would hold in court in the long run. In fact, multiple other smuggling cases were settled without ever being heard in court. Five of the indictments in the Harquahala Valley case—in addition to three that were disposed of from the outset due to a lack of evidence—were dismissed for undisclosed reasons.[4] Of the 51 indicted border crossers, 15 were initially set to go to trial, but many of those charges were also dismissed or the accused were allowed to plea to lesser offenses. The only indictment that culminated in a jury trial was that of the driver—an irregular migrant himself who had volunteered to drive the vehicle in return for a discount on his smuggling fee. He was sentenced to a three-year suspended sentence term and immediately deported. In a separate case also pertaining to charges under the Coyote Law, four out of five indicted border crossers were allowed to plea to minor charges on the day before the trial was to commence, while the fifth detainee, who could also have benefited from the offer, had been deported earlier that week, apparently by accident (Kiefer 2006).

The high number of cases settled suggests that the intention behind the statute's enforcement and alternate interpretation was never one of punishing migrants with lengthy incarceration terms. Instead, it became an effective tactic to generate a substantial number of successful convictions over a very short period of time, which conveyed a sense of efficiency of local law enforcement agencies—in this case, the Maricopa County Sheriff's Office—while also conveying an increased sense of urgency surrounding the need to control irregular migration.

In the months that followed the Harquahala Valley case, the Coyote Law continued to be used as an effective mechanism of immigration control and migrant criminalization. Less than a year after Thomas's decision to charge extralegal border crossers arrested in Maricopa County with co-conspiring to commit their own smuggling, his office celebrated the one-thousandth indictment under the smuggling statute with an official press release (Thomas 2009). Between January of 2008 and November of 2013, the number of convictions increased to 1641

(Stern 2009). No mention was made of how many of those convicted were irregular migrants, or how many had actually been determined as human smuggling facilitators. Over the years, few of those charged under the Coyote Law ever opted to take their case to trial, fearing lengthy court processes or harsher sentences. SB1372 was highly effective at prosecuting those "who were the easiest to apprehend and least able to defend themselves" (Tucson Citizen 2006), and at furthering the sense of impending crisis over irregular migration in the state.

Conclusion

By the end of the first decade of the new millennium, Arizona gained international notoriety with the passage of strict anti-immigrant laws. Multiple pieces of legislation aimed at directly impacting the presence of Latino residents in the state were approved by the state congress and signed into law. Local and state enforcement agencies, by entering into agreements with the federal government, held wide-ranging powers in the area of immigration law enforcement and control. Together, the legislation and the policing practices that were put into place were effective at communicating a heightened sense of concern over the presence of Latinos (especially those of Mexican origin) in Arizona. As it stood, this rhetoric constructed Latinos as foreigners, inherently unauthorized and criminal.

Yet Arizona's history of anti-immigrant sentiment is not new. A history of structural, race-based inequality has shaped the experiences of generations of families of Mexican origin in the state. Institutional racism and discriminatory measures have historically limited the social, political and economic opportunities available to people of color in Arizona, and created the conditions for their ensuing marginalization.

Following changes in federal border control policy in the mid-1990s that intentionally sought to redirect extralegal border crossing flows into Arizona, the state became the main point of entry for irregular border crossers along the US–Mexico divide (Cornelius 2001, 2005; Cornelius and Lewis 2006; Rubio-Goldsmith et al. 2006). Fearing encounters with immigration authorities, undocumented migrants shifted their routes into the Arizona desert, heading into the most remote, hot and dry regions of the desert borderlands (Martinez et al. 2013, 11), where they were particularly vulnerable to the elements. Within a decade, federal policy and enforcement along the border had led to the deaths of thousands of irregular border crossers in the Arizona desert (Rubio-Goldsmith et al. 2006; Goldsmith and Romero 2008; O'Leary and Sanchez 2011).

Yet one of the least explored implications of these measures relates to the emergence of the local human smuggling market. Extended families on both sides of the US–Mexico border, sharing their own resources and personal connections, began to guide extralegal border crossers into Arizona following the implementation of Operation Hold the Line and Gatekeeper along other sections of the border. While extralegal border crossings were not new to Arizona, the state's emergence as a border crossing point was the result of enforcement measures aimed at controlling immigration flows.

Criminalization efforts aimed at controlling smuggling operations emerged in the mid-2000s, allegedly as an effort to prevent border crossers' exploitation at the hands of human smugglers. The passage of SB1372 into law and its enforcement, however, had no impact at reducing migrants' victimization. If anything, it became another tool that allowed for the application of racial profiling and justified additional efforts in policing and surveillance of Latino residents in the state.

Until 2013, the majority of the smuggling-related convictions in the state had involved the charging of extralegal border crossers with conspiring to commit their own human smuggling; very few involved the conviction of human smuggling facilitators themselves. This trend is not unique. Most smuggling cases globally similarly lead to the arrest of migrants and refugees, rather than those facilitating their journeys. As the case of Arizona shows, the criminalization of border crossing constitutes the element driving facilitators to devise alternative means to further reduce the likelihood of their detection while en route, leading to the reliance on more dangerous crossing routes. But the prevalence of border crossers among those convicted for smuggling may actually be an indicator of changes within the structure of smuggling and, most importantly, of the relationship between facilitators and their clients, where the legal risks connected with facilitating extralegal border crossings are transferred from the facilitators to border crossers, this way avoiding detention.

The following chapters turn their attention to the everyday activities in which local residents of Phoenix engage in the provision of extralegal border crossings, delving into their experiences not merely as facilitators, but as members of immigrant communities, their lives also impacted by structural discrimination and violence.

Notes

1 According to the National Conference of State Legislatures database, 413 bills related to policing and enforcing immigration laws have been approved in the US since 2013. See www.ncsl.org/research/immigration/immigration-laws-database.aspx.

2 According to estimates compiled by the Pima County Office of the Medical Examiner (PCOMO), between 1990 and 2013, a total of 2238 human remains were recovered in the Arizona desert. When measured against Border Patrol Apprehension Statistics, this number indicates that the death rate of irregular border crossers began to increase exponentially in 1999 (Martinez et al. 2013, 15) and continued to escalate during the first decade of the twenty-first century, even as apprehension numbers decreased. During that decade, Arizona became the most lethal area among all border crossing points. About 45 percent of the fatalities have been determined to be related to exposure to the elements. The overwhelming majority of those who died were men between the ages of 20 and 29 (Martinez et al. 2013, 16–17).

3 We Are America/Somos America Coalition of Arizona et al v. Maricopa County Board of Supervisors, et al. 2:06-cv-02816-RCB District of Arizona (Phoenix Division) 11/21/2006.

4 The legal case file pertaining to the first prosecution under the Coyote Law describes the cases of men suffering from medical conditions that could be worsened due to lack of treatment. It is inferred that these individuals were not detained due to concerns over liability and were instead released to the immigration service for immediate deportation.

3 "Together as a family"

The nature and structure of smuggling

I first interviewed suspect number 1, identified as Juan Torres Sanchez from Chalchicomula, Mexico. I asked him how he got here, and he told some friends [sic]. Juan told me there were initially three of them, but soon they hooked up with two more and all five then traveled together to get to the border. I asked him who he contacted to get across; he said they just came to the border and got [together] with some other people to cross. When asked where he crossed he told me he really didn't know, [that] he wasn't familiar with this area, and so he really couldn't tell me where they crossed. I asked him who had led them across the border, and he said he didn't know, [that] they just came across as a group.

(Hernandez 2006, 6)

I asked Antonio Serdan, suspect number 33, if there was a coyote who crossed with the group but he said there wasn't. I asked him how much it was going to cost him to cross the border, and he told me it wasn't costing anything. I asked him to tell me what he meant. He said they got together back in Mexico and decided to share the cost. I asked how those responsible for the vehicles were going to make their money, or if it was going to be free and he said no, it wasn't going to be free. I asked him to explain [that] to me . . . and said they were only going to pay whatever they could afford, whatever they had on them. I asked him about those who didn't have any money on them, and he said others were going to chip in. He told me they were helping each other out—like a family.

(Maricopa County v. Salazar-Hernandez 2006)

On March 2, 2006, officers from multiple law enforcement agencies in Arizona descended upon Harquahala Valley to interview what would become the first group of extralegal border crossers to be indicted under SB1372, the Coyote Law. The task in itself was challenging, as the above quotes reflect. There were only a limited number of Spanish-speaking officers at hand and all 54 detainees had to be processed in time for their initial court appearance a few hours later. A decision was made to pair and to provide the officers with a set of specific questions to ask.

The questions involved a series of assumptions commonly held around smuggling. It assumed most of those detained were of Mexican origin and that their transit was the result of an agreement with a smuggling facilitator, established via a monetary exchange. It was also assumed that they all traveled to a specific destination—and for the same reason (finding employment). The answers provided would eventually be used in court to demonstrate the existence of a conspiracy between the smuggling facilitator and the detainee to commit an act of human smuggling. The questions asked to the detainees were as follows:

1   Name and date of birth
2   Where do you live in Mexico?/Where were you from in Mexico?
3   Where, how or with whom did you arrange to get into the United States?
4   How much did you pay or how much do you still owe for your transportation to the US?
5   Where were you going?
6   Who were you meeting with?
7   Do you have work here?

Quotes like the two introducing this chapter attest to the immediate challenges – and the frustrations—faced by the officers. Most detainees were from Mexico, and at the time of their arrest were en route to multiple cities along the US West Coast. But that was where the similarities ended, and the questions soon began to reveal their own limitations. The impromptu questionnaire reflected the perceptions of law enforcement authorities surrounding smuggling processes, not the experiences of those traveling. The questions fell short of identifying the diversity of experiences, routes, arrangements and expectations of those in transit, and the complexity of the relationships that existed among those seeking to cross the border extralegally.

Some migrants had traveled on their own. Some had befriended other travelers along the way, eventually deciding to travel together for protection and support without the help of a guide or coyote. Others had contacted a godparent, childhood friend or classmate in their hometown to facilitate their journey, while others had found crossing assistance somewhere along the border. Some had entered into financial arrangements in anticipation of their crossing; some had in fact already made payments. But many others were unaware of the cost of their journey, this having been negotiated by older siblings or parents. And while some knew their destinations, others simply hoped the crossing would be successful enough for them to get "somewhere." Friends or family members residing in the US would pay for some, while others would pay for their own once they had found a job, or had been working along the way to pay off their fee.

Most of these journeys challenged conventional narratives of smuggling—that of the carefully planned travels facilitated by large, professional criminal networks and based on exploitative financial terms. Instead, family ties, individual decision-making and the support of friends, distant family members or even complete strangers, combined with the assistance of smuggling facilitators, were what made these journeys successful—or at least somewhat effective. The majority of extralegal border crossings tend to follow a rather different logic from that of law enforcement. While somewhat organized, crossings are largely informal, often unsuccessful, reliant upon individual perceptions of risk and safety, coincidence and, in the words of those who have successfully crossed the divide, "a little luck." As Agustin Alvarez and Jose Galindo described it:

> You never know what you are going to get. Sometimes you end up in the hands of a good coyote, who takes care of you; others you get caught by *la migra*[1] right away; other times you find good comrades and the journey just goes smoothly. It is . . . like a chain.

In the case of the men and women of Harquahala Valley, the effort had been unsuccessful, but not worthless. The group had crossed in the manner in which they had envisioned it: as a group, supporting one another—or, as one of those interviewed put it, as "a family."

How can this combination of uncertainty, chaos and luck lead to successful crossings?

Human smuggling has been primarily defined in international conventions as a deviant, morally heinous act—as "a crime involving the procurement for financial or other material benefit of illegal entry of a person into a State of which that person is not a national or resident" (UNODC 2013), or as "a growing global crime that exposes thousands of migrants to unacceptable risks and challenges the integrity of international borders" (IOM 2013). After 9/11, it became a "transnational issue that threatens national security alongside clandestine terrorist travel and trafficking in persons" (State Department 2013). This series of characterizations (smuggling as a global crime, a national security concern and an act of financial exploitation) has consistently failed to capture the day-to-day roles migrants and refugees play in carving their own pathways to mobility, as well as the elements of collaboration and support that characterize extralegal border crossings.

This chapter documents the nature and the structure of smuggling from the perspectives of the men and women who facilitate them, and from those who rely on their services. It draws from first-hand testimonies and in-court narratives of smuggling cases to identify the factors that smugglers and border crossers recognize as central to the provision of successful extralegal border crossings. Through the views of its actors, smuggling emerges not as a calculated for-profit operation, but as a haphazard, often unsystematic, community-based, collective effort toward mobility—a process that affords income-generating opportunities to some of the most marginalized residents along the migrant trails. Smuggling activities emerge, therefore, for both border crossers and smuggling facilitators, as a legitimate effort at maintaining and restoring their personal dignity and integrity in the face of marginality.

Privileging facilitators' understandings of smuggling destabilizes the state's perceived role as the single agent for determining what constitutes legitimate forms of labor and what ought to be criminalized (Heyman 1999, in Galemba 2012a, 2008). Furthermore, the recognition of smuggling facilitators' own conceptualizations of their roles and activities demonstrates how the notion of work, while "culturally and politically codified," can be "subject[ed] to reinterpretation, resistance and reformulation" (Ortner 2006, 7). This chapter examines the ways in which the men and women who participate in smuggling, whether as facilitators or border crossers, organize and work together in an effort to reduce the impact of the processes of structural inequality and disenfranchisement processes historically impacting Latino migrants in the US Southwest.

The "informal" as "illicit"; the illicit as work

An increasing number of social scientists have begun to examine how illegalized activities create multiple opportunities for labor, recognizing that it is the state that at first creates the very conditions of illegality and informality which allow these employment practices to flourish (Galemba 2008, 22). Criminological inquiries into border violence have also paid much-needed critical attention to border policing and to the ways in which it has allowed for illicit practices to flourish, impacting the lives of those who travel extralegally. Structural violence of this kind creates room for the emergence of actions to resist, change and even violate the limitations it imposes upon agency—or in this case, mobility (Spener 2009b). Efforts to research the ways in which those who live on the margins of the formal and informal economies devise forms of labor to bridge and blur these licit and illicit divides (Nordstrom 2007; Ferguson 2006; Galemba 2008, 21) have emerged. This chapter therefore examines how irregular migrants in Arizona working as facilitators of extralegal border crossings conceptualize their involvement as legitimate and their actions as valid and necessary forms of labor in the context of a structurally violent border defined by policing and control.

At the same time, one must be careful not to interpret smugglers' actions as successful efforts at curtailing oppression or at generating deep structural change. Some smuggling journeys are in fact characterized by extreme, yet highly specific forms of violence and exploitation (Kyle and Scarcelli 2009); the risk of or potential for harm is real (O'Leary 2008). And most importantly, one should keep in mind that smuggling facilitators' actions contribute to the maintenance of the neoliberal project by often assisting large numbers of refugees and migrants of color to enter the economic system that relies on the availability of individuals willing to accept low-paying jobs. The success of the contemporary nation-state depends on the reproduction of these very mechanisms of economic oppression. And so while smuggling is, on the one hand, a tool in the effort to create mechanisms for mobility and for the sustenance of marginalized communities, it can also allow for the perpetuation of inequality and the display of violence against the most vulnerable of border crossers. Yet human smuggling still provides those marginalized by the state with an opportunity to counteract some of the barriers to equality they face by becoming agents of mobility within a neoliberal economy that constrains and criminalizes them at times, but which also depends on their labor for its survival.

In this sense, the testimonies of the everyday lives of human smuggling facilitators in Maricopa County and their own perceptions of their activities constitute, rather than simple data on illicit activities, evidence of how people along borders have found ways to challenge "the rigid definitions of legality" (Galemba 2008, 20) and redefine the meaning of labor in the global age.

"Profiling" the smuggler

Overall, what characterized the men and women in this research was the ordinariness of their lives. There was no single or specific profile of a smuggler or factors predicting an individual's likely involvement in smuggling. Those working at facilitating extralegal border crossings in Arizona came from rural and urban areas from Mexico, the Caribbean and Central America, the same way they were from communities with and without a tradition of US-bound migration. Their ages ranged widely—from teenagers seeking to cross the border for the first time to elderly men and women supporting themselves with the income generated from occasionally housing border crossers in transit.

While both men and women participate in smuggling activities, their roles have a tendency to be gendered. Men were overrepresented and were more likely to be identified as smugglers, whereas women, while also active, were less likely to be among those arrested in the context of anti-human smuggling operations. Women were also more prone to have lived in the country for longer periods of time than their male counterparts, who at the time of their arrest reported having lived in the country only for short periods of time or seasonally. Most men lived outside Arizona but traveled to the state with the sole purpose of participating in smuggling, while women had a tendency to operate in their immediate communities.

Some facilitators were formally educated—a man from Cuba reported being a business school graduate and a man from Mexico had a degree in education—while others hardly knew how to read or write. Some had US-born children and spouses, while others supported families abroad. For the majority, their arrest had taken place in the context of their first attempt to enter the US, having accepted to conduct a specific smuggling task in exchange for a discount in their fees. Only a few facilitators had a long history of involvement in smuggling (this was particularly the case among the women). But most facilitators participated only occasionally, mostly during times of financial need or temporary unemployment.

Amid their diversity, the facilitators shared important commonalities. In terms of their immigration status, most were irregular migrants.[2] The majority were of Mexican origin, although participation was not restricted to a specific nationality (there were men and women from El Salvador, Nicaragua, Guatemala and Cuba, although in much smaller numbers). Most facilitators were working-class individuals, members of low-income families in their countries of origin, and who had migrated to support their families or to improve their own quality of life. With the exception of migrants who became involved in smuggling to finance their own journeys, most participants in the smuggling market in Maricopa County were employed full-time. Their schedules (several of them worked two or even three jobs) often limited the amount of time they had for smuggling activities, deriving from their participation in what constituted only a supplemental form of income. Full-time involvement in smuggling was virtually non-existent among those interviewed. With few exceptions, facilitators had no criminal backgrounds (and when present, crimes were of a lesser nature, involving petty offenses and traffic violations in the majority); not a single one reported, or was found to have, ties to transnational criminal organizations.

Most facilitators worked alongside friends and family members, relying on shared resources. Facilitators often reflected on the practice's role as a form of solidarity and cooperation, carried out on behalf of family members and friends. Most facilitators operated by assisting members of their immediate circles; hierarchies were virtually non-existent, with most simply working independently. These factors challenge commonly held perceptions of smuggling as hierarchically organized, violent or profit-driven, being instead rooted in social interactions and notions of collaboration, support and protection.

Open participation

Smuggling organizations are frequently portrayed as having a closed membership, limited to highly trusted individuals. It is also common to come across anecdotal accounts of initiation, rituals or codes governing such membership. Testimonies suggest instead a much more flexible structure, where anyone—including actual clients—is able to join a smuggling effort by contributing time or resources to ensure the success of a crossing.

That was the case of Roberto Amezcua. During a crossing journey, a group of coyotes lost a driver to an arrest. Having a group of migrants needing to reach their destination, the facilitators asked their clients for help:

> One of the coyotes asked us if anyone knew how to drive, and I raised my hand and said I did. The coyotes offered to reduce my fee to $2000 if I drove one of the vehicles. They gave me a radio and I was taken to a location where I picked up ten people. The coyotes were telling me where to drive, but I was pulled over [by police] for a traffic violation. I am not a smuggler, I was only offered to drive a van.

Allegiance or membership to a specific group was not required, as most participants worked on an ad hoc basis, their roles determined and agreed upon on a one-on-one, as-needed basis. Most facilitators simply join smuggling efforts conducted by friends or family members or by invitation, their participation seen often as a familial obligation. Annette Rodriguez commented:

> What we do is not wrong. I first started doing this because my boyfriend's daughter needed help to cross her own two little girls—she had not seen them for over a year. I felt the obligation to help; it did not cost me anything. I just went with her to pick up the children and we came back. We are family, we must support each other.

Flexibility

Among smuggling's participants, the flexibility of the activity, given its non-constant demands, constitutes one of the main reasons for involvement:

The good thing about "the business" is that I do not need to work around the clock. I do this [participate in human smuggling] whenever my cousin has people to cross. But the rest of the time I just do my regular job. I clean houses during the day time. I have a small house-cleaning business and that keeps me very busy. But whenever she needs my help I make time to help her. That one time I got arrested I was in fact on my way to work. I was going to clean a house.

As Zhang and Chin (2003) uncovered while conducting research among Chinese human smugglers, smuggling participants have a large tendency to be employed (or self-employed) full-time, with many of them holding second and even third jobs. The provision of extralegal border crossings is driven by demand; what then results is a practice primarily of sporadic, occasional nature, often requiring only temporary involvement on the part of its facilitators. Most participants in fact welcomed the flexibility and convenience of smuggling as the main factors leading to their participation. They commented on the flexible schedules and seasonal nature of smuggling, and how these allowed them to remain employed year-round:

I work at a resort as a gardener for most of the year. But then there are times when the resort does not need us so they cut down my hours. This is usually when the hot weather arrives. I ask the foreman for permission, and he lays me off for a few months. That is the time when I go and work passing people; when the foreman needs me back at the resort, I just go back to work.

Limited stigma

There is ample recognition of the illicit nature of human smuggling among its participants. Yet the women and men in this study repeatedly characterized their contributions to border crossing as legitimate forms of labor, conducted on behalf of others who needed help. Facilitators refuse to frame their work as a criminal activity. A female facilitator explained:

I get mad when I hear how people say we are criminals. I work hard to give my children what they need. I work all week at my regular job and then on the weekends I go to the border and cross children. Yes, I know this is not legal, but from there to say that what I do is a crime . . . I help people. I have always considered my job that of helping people. And I am proud of what I do. I do not like it when reporters say it is a crime—in my mind it is not.

Furthermore, among facilitators human smuggling carries significantly less stigma than other occupations, like drug trafficking or sex work. While earnings are typically not as high as those available in other illicit markets, smuggling facilitators did not have to fear the increased level of surveillance or violence that is connected to drug transportation and sales, and their families are not subjected to criticism or shame. As one interviewee observed during a visit at her place of employment:

> Well, as you can see, we are not rich. We work hard. My sister and I own the salon and do an honest job here every day cutting hair. I [would] much rather be poor than risk my life like other people do—like those who join the mafia or who work with them. Sometimes we get invited to their parties, but I don't really like to go. Some have nice homes and all but they don't even know what to do with the things they have. And sometimes you know, they just get mad and kill each other. So I just work hard, do some [smuggling] jobs every now and then, and just live my life. Bringing people over won't get me killed.

Emphasis on collaboration and solidarity

A common element in smuggling narratives was the notion of collaboration. Facilitators work alongside each other to support specific segments of a journey, thus sharing income-generating opportunities. Yet rather than an emphasis on finances, there were constant references to the community-based nature of smuggling, interactions with friends and family members and examples of generosity on behalf of those in need.

A common element within the narratives was solidarity, often explained as the sharing of income opportunities extended to members of the community whose financial situations are perceived as dire:

> I knew a woman working at my hotel who had a disabled baby boy. The baby needed special care, and my coworker was working the night shift so that she could spend the day with her son, but then suddenly her hours at the hotel got cut, and she had to get another job passing out flyers during the daytime. I felt sorry for her because she could not take care of the boy and told her I could connect her with someone who could pay her a bit of money if she housed a few people at her apartment every once in a while. She was most grateful.

Leadership and structure

With counted exceptions, human smuggling groups lack identifiable command or leadership structures (Zhang 2007, 95). Neither the case files nor the informants provided conclusive statements in regard to the existence of a single, centralized power providing operational or logistical support in any of the smuggling groups identified. Instead facilitators acted on their own behalf, or as a favor to whoever requested their services. In other words, facilitators acted independently, or in coordination with their peers, but never under any kind of leadership. "I don't have a boss, I work for myself and I know what I have to do," a female facilitator expressed, showing how participants value the independence that comes from their involvement in smuggling.

It was also common for facilitators not to know the names or location of each person in the "chain" of steps needed for a crossing to be successful, most knowing only the name of the person who executed the prior task, or the one of the relative or friend who alerted them to the opportunity. This factor may act as a protective mechanism—in the event that a crossing operation is detected by police, those detained would be unable to provide exact information or names of others involved[3]—but also constitutes further evidence of the absence of leadership or centralized command.

Competition

The human smuggling market is far from monolithic. Crossings were provided by facilitators organized in multiple fashions, almost always relying on the assistance of those living in the same neighborhood or household. As explained by a driver:

> Sometimes I pick up people on my own; others I call [a coordinator] to see if she needs help; other people call me and ask if I am available to work. We just help each other out. Sometimes you work with people, others you do it on your own. You just never know. But here there is no envy: we all have our people we cross.

Extralegal border crossers are not facilitated by a single kind of group or facilitator. Rather, it appeared some groups and even individuals are simply more effective at transporting border crossers in transit than others by virtue of their access to resources—which can include bigger and faster vehicles, or access to specific routes and to more experienced guides or walkers. Yet none of these logistical advantages translated into market dominance and, quite surprisingly, did not seem to generate or respond to competition. While some facilitators focused on the provision of specialized crossings,[4] no single group appeared to dominate or control the market. Instead, facilitators worked within their own social circles, and in that sense served specific groups of border crossers, thereby virtually eliminating the need to compete over clientele. As a facilitator explained:

> We only work with people we know. We do not accept people from the outside, strangers. It is too risky. So we only bring people across who are referred to us from people who have already traveled with us, nobody else. It is less of a problem that way.

Indeed, there was limited indication of facilitators competing for the same clients. In fact, they frequently referred border crossers to other facilitators when unable to provide a service or when the border crosser required specialized care or services (as in the case of children, the elderly or those who are mobility impaired). A woman, speaking about her coyote, commented:

> We arranged the crossing from home, and [the recruiter] sent us to someone who was just having a very hard time getting us across. So I called [the recruiter] and told him what was going on. He called the other guy, who then took us to another man who was able to cross us right away. Everybody was very kind.

This level of sharing further reduced competition, strengthened ties among facilitators and built collaboration and trust overall. While complex crossings were often the result of facilitators having access to significant resources, it was ultimately the work of individual facilitators that allowed for the efficient provision of services, and not a group's specific size. Having access to multiple facilitators may make the difference between a failed and a successful border crossing project.

Irregular planning and execution

Smugglers often faced sudden changes and had limited ability to control the conditions encountered during the facilitation of a journey. Accordingly, smuggling's execution tended to be quite informal, even erratic at times (Zhang 2007, 99).

The collaborations on extralegal border crossings were always established among individual facilitators, and tended to be temporary, informal and sporadic – in response to the fluctuating nature of the demand for smuggling services. Collaborations were negotiated as verbal agreements between friends or relatives who requested "favors" from one another and who committed to assist only for the duration of a particular crossing. Favors ranged from the performance of individual tasks, like driving or check-cashing services, to housing migrants in transit for a few days. A single collaboration could lead to further opportunities, but this offer was never guaranteed or made explicit.

Collaborations were carefully planned to the extent that facilitators kept each other informed and expected the other parties involved to do their jobs. Invitations to participate were usually extended only to people who had access to resources and had proven to be reliable. Yet while immigrant journeys may appear to involve a linear trajectory, crossings hardly ever follow a specific order. Rather, they are adapted to the conditions of the field. The degree of law enforcement surveillance may be high, drivers may not be available or the demand for services may vary. Plans must often change in order to accommodate fluctuations in the weather, an indisposed or injured immigrant, and potential encounters with police officers or even groups of the feared *bajadores*—bandits known to steal human cargo from facilitators.

Limited use of technology

In his work on smuggling along the US–Mexico border, Andreas has consistently argued that smuggling operations have shifted from being traditional family enterprises to highly complex organizations. He suggests that increased smuggling fees also allow smuggling groups to acquire state-of-the-art equipment to consolidate their wealth and power (Andreas 2001, 117–119).

It is important to keep in mind that facilitators operate independently, relying on resources immediately available to them. None of the cases analyzed in this sample yielded evidence of facilitators using sophisticated equipment or resources. Instead cell phones—highly affordable in the era of global communication—and short-wave radios, used in remote desert areas, constituted the extent of their technological prowess. Facilitators' reliance on technology was no different from that of any other cell phone or internet user. The use of cell phones and radios is therefore extensive due to their affordability, and by no means should this be interpreted as a synonym of technological advancement or organizational progress.

Arizona's facilitators were far from achieving the level of complexity to which Andreas refers. In fact, smuggling operators carried out successful crossings often on the basis of pure ingenuity. The structure of smuggling (as divided into multiple, specialized tasks) leads to fees being split among larger numbers of participants, further reducing the concentration of profits and the likelihood of most facilitators accumulating or develop any kind of wealth. Profits are immediately recycled in the local economy, and hardly ever saved in order to further invest in one's participation in smuggling. Simplicity and flexibility were key.

Community-based nature

The cases analyzed reveal the fundamental role community plays in the enduring nature of smuggling operations. As previously discussed, the majority of the literature on smuggling emphasizes the business aspect of the practice and tends to focus on the financial transactions that take place among facilitators and their clients. Most respondents explained their participation in smuggling as involving more than carefully calculated profit equations. For many facilitators, the social prestige that comes from being a trustworthy guide or driver, or from securing safe accommodation for women and children in transit, is more valuable than the generation of financial returns, as social recognition can be used as leverage to secure other goods or services within the local community post-transit.

Given smugglers' reliance on their own groups of friends and relatives, compliance dominates the execution of transits; it is expected that facilitators will provide care and safety during the journey of the migrant, his or her wellbeing ensured even when in the most precarious of conditions. Amalia Lopez shared her experience of the smuggling groups behind the crossing of her youngest child—a teenager:

> I told the smuggler: "I know you. I know who you are. We are from the same town. So let me tell you. I put my son in your hands. If anything, and I do mean anything happens to him, I will find you!" [Laughs] But the truth is that those kids—they were very young—took very good care of my son. I went with them for my son because they were the ones who crossed me the last time I crossed, and they were always very kind, very well mannered. They had even taken us to church to pray for a successful crossing.

Border crossers and their families serve as sources of referrals and references, and often hide the identity of the facilitator in the event of an arrest. Yet whenever protections are not afforded, and border crossers (whether acquaintances, friends or relatives) are mistreated, abused or scammed, they show no hesitation in reporting the identity of the facilitator to the authorities or to future or potential clients.

Division of labor in smuggling

One characteristic of smuggling is the highly defined nature of its tasks. Defined by Zhang (2008) as specialization, border crossings are divided into multiple tasks. Each facilitator is in charge of performing a specific activity connected with a specific aspect of the crossing—such as driving, collecting fees, obtaining vehicles, guiding groups through the desert or acting as a lookout. Substitutions may occur, and a facilitator may jump in to cover for someone who is absent or otherwise unable to perform a specific task, but almost always returns to perform their originally assigned portion of the crossing activity. Intermingling of tasks is also limited. A woman who worked alongside her husband explained this process:

> There was a time when one of the [drivers] that take people into Phoenix got sick, and so my husband was asked to substitute for him. Because driving is a different kind of work, he got paid more than what he did when he just picked up wire transfers. When the driver['s health] improved my husband just went back to do what he always used to do.

The number of people involved in facilitating border crossings is primarily dependent on the context of each journey (number of border crossers; time of day; weather conditions; level of surveillance, etc.). Crossings are not linear; they do not follow a specific trajectory or route every time. However, there are a series of tasks that appear to be common to most crossings. These typically include recruitment, guidance, transportation, housing and financial services (the collection and disbursement of payments and fees). These tasks in turn create specific labor opportunities for drivers, coordinators, lookouts, helpers, and guards, to name a few.

The roles described below reflect some of the tasks performed by smuggling facilitators in Maricopa County. These categories may not represent each and every one of the activities involved in smuggling, but they account for the roles often reported by the participants in the current study and are also identified in legal case files. As a reminder, the order in which the tasks are listed is not intended to suggest extralegal border crossings follow a linear trajectory—a guide may be needed during multiple stages of the journey, and more than one driver may be involved in facilitating the transportation of a traveler, for example. In most cases, the role is described using the name given by the smuggling facilitators themselves.

Recruiters

Enganchadores are in charge of recruiting potential clients. Like most human smuggling facilitators, recruiters usually work independently, identifying and soliciting potential clients and receiving a commission for each person recruited. Recruiters rely primarily on their immediate social circles to identify likely travelers—that is, they tend to conduct recruitment activities among their own relatives, former colleagues or the children of friends and neighbors, usually by extending personal invitations to rely on their services. Marina Herrera explained:

> I had a friend who had moved to the States when I was younger, and one day she called to ask if I was interested in coming to *El Otro Lado*.[5] I said "yes, but I do not have the resources." So she said she would help me with the money, but that I had to be ready whenever she told me, and that I could pay her in installments later, once I got a job. She took care of everything for me. And a few days later she called to let me know everything was ready, and to just go to Mexico City and catch a flight for Tijuana, that somebody would get me from there.

Most recruiters are known to those who travel with them. They tend to be close friends or relatives, referred to them from former clients, or individuals known to have crossed the border successfully in the past and who rely on their experience to guide people safely across the border. Therefore, far from being unsavory characters, recruiters tend to be highly trusted individuals due to their level of social proximity and are rarely perceived as abusive, coercive or demanding. In this project, recruiters ranged from godmothers and childhood friends to former neighbors, even older siblings:

> Laurencio traveled with William, Lorena and Crisoforo who he knew were also undocumented illegal aliens [sic] planning to enter the United States illegally. When asked, Laurencio said he knew that William, Lorena and Crisoforo had made an agreement with their godmother Luisa who lives in Chicago to be smuggled into the United States for an unknown fee. Furthermore, he knew [that the siblings] would have to repay Luisa back [sic] once [they had] found employment in Chicago.
>
> (Maricopa County v. Gonzalez-Tagal 2007, p. 4)

Entering into smuggling agreements with known recruiters is often believed to reduce risk and to increase the likelihood of a successful journey—that is, one that culminates in a successful border crossing. It also establishes an expectation that, on the basis of a pre-existing relationship, the border crosser will be protected during the journey, provided with care when needed and never mistreated. In this sense, the kinds of journeys facilitated by a reliable smuggler tend to be perceived as the safest, and it is highly sought after by those seeking to travel without harm. When questioned in court about the particulars of his journey, Gerardo Garcia expressed his confidence in the arrangements secured by his friend on his behalf:

> Gerardo had made arrangements with a friend of his named Cesar to help him enter the United States illegally. Gerardo stated that his friend Cesar new [sic] of a man that could help him (Gerardo) cross over into the United States for a fee

of $2500. Gerardo stated [that] he and his friend Cesar came to an agreement that once Gerardo found employment in the United States he would [pay] Cesar back the $2500 dollars [sic] for the coyote. Gerardo stated [that] once the agreement was in place his friend Cesar made all the arrangements for him to be crossed into the United States . . . Gerardo stated [that] once he arriving to [sic] California or Oregon he would start to send payments back to his friend Cesar as agreed upon.

(Maricopa County v. Diaz-Cisneros, 2007, p. 3)

A second kind of recruitment activity often takes place along key points of a journey—borders, checkpoints, ports and other places of departure, like train or bus stations. Recruiters approach potential clients who may be looking for assistance with their crossing, and offer their services:

Ricardo left his hometown and traveled to the border for the sole purpose of entering the United States illegally to see his daughter. While on the border he made arrangements with an unknown male they called "Jose" or "Cangrejo" to be smuggled into the United States for a fee of $1900. Jose approached Ricardo at the station, where he offered his services.

This form of recruitment often involves considerable risk to the traveler, who, contrary to the typical experience with the first kind of *enganchador*, lacks any background knowledge of the individual offering services and cannot always effectively mobilize assistance if things go wrong. In most cases, those seeking to cross borders tend to altogether avoid this kind of recruitment arrangement. The lack of a personal social relationship between client and recruiter tends to result in the absence of social obligations or expectations connected to the smuggling journey and increases the risk for the traveler of being scammed. Most often those impacted by smuggling-related violence or scams are those who hire smugglers who are unknown to them, although acts of violence can potentially take place with any kind of facilitator. The testimony of a man involved in a kidnapping case identified in this study reveals some of the abuses that may occur when hiring strangers to provide border crossing assistance:

I traveled from Chihuahua to Agua Prieta just to cross. I crossed the border with a small group of people. There I contacted a coyote and I agreed to pay him some money to guide me through the desert and to take me to Phoenix. I had not paid for my transportation. We walked in the desert for two days and then I was picked up by a truck and taken to Phoenix. While at the drop house, there were seven other people like myself. There were also three other coyotes watching us. They took our shoes, passports and money and locked us up in a small room. The coyotes hit me and the others several times and were very abusive to all of us. We were given food and water only once a day and it was never enough. The coyotes also increased the amount that I was supposed to pay. I had to call my aunt so that she could pay the $2200 fee.

*Guides (*guías *or* caminadores*)*

The activities associated with walking border crossers to and across the border while avoiding detection are the work of guides (*caminadores*, or walkers in Spanish). Guides are often long-term residents of border regions, familiar with the desert landscape. Their tasks involve leading groups of border crossers through sections of the desert to predetermined pick-up points where they meet with drivers. Guides, through their awareness of roads and trails, identify resting or hiding points. They are also reported to carry food, water and first aid kits to assist those in transit, and are usually equipped with radios and cell phones that allow them to communicate with other guides and lookouts, or to summon help in the event of an emergency. *Caminadores* usually work in pairs, often training younger guides (known in some instances as *ayudantes*, or "helpers"):

> We usually send two *caminadores* and a helper. They have radios and that is how they communicate. The *ayudante* makes sure there are no *migras* nearby, tells the *caminador* when to wait or when to go onward. A *caminador* or an *ayudante* can wait with someone who is not doing well or fell behind, or call for help when needed. Sometimes you just can't move the groups, because there is too much surveillance, and so the guides also decide when it is time for everybody to come back to the hotel, and when things get better we try again.

Guides often appear in narratives of border crossings as malevolent and ill intentioned (Isacson et al. 2013). Scholars have documented cases of guides lying to border crossers on the distances they would walk; of abandoning border crossers in the desert without water; of sexually harassing women; and of robbing clients once they have reached isolated parts of the journey (O'Leary 2009).

While the presence of petty criminals and the very involvement of guides in these actions along the migrant trail cannot be denied, guides are not the only ones involved in the victimization of clients. As Hagan (2008) and Spener (2004) have documented, most guides do provide effective guidance and company; and their awareness of migrant trails often means that clients are likely to travel shorter distances than if traveling alone. Walkers also decide when journeys are risky to attempt and whether they should be canceled or postponed. They are often known to stay behind with an injured or ailing border crosser, or to secure medical or rescue assistance in an emergency. Guides reportedly walk those who are unable to keep up with the group to designated meeting points from where they can either be taken back across the border to recover before the next crossing attempt, or be easily found by Border Patrol officers (Spener 2009a). Honduras, a teenage guide, reported:

> Once I was leading a group with a lady I knew right away would have trouble making it. She had hypertension, and once we started walking she was unable to keep up with the group. I then decided we could not move forward. We all headed back. She stayed for a couple days at the hotel to recover. I was not going to risk her life that way. I get mad when people say we just leave clients behind; we are not that kind of people.

In her work on spirituality on the border crossing, Hagan (2008) documented cases of guides who prayed with their groups prior to embarking on desert treks, and who apologized to their clients in advance for any discomfort or challenge they might encounter along the journey. Caring and dependable guides are in fact treasured by border crossers, who are aware of the challenges surrounding their crossings:

> I met these other guys on the bus on the way to Agua Prieta, and we became friends. They seemed to know who we were supposed to go meet with. Once we reached the border, they introduced me to Fernando, a dark-skin male of about 23 and kind of tall who guided groups of *indocumentados*[6] through Arizona. Fernando only crossed people with references. But he had helped people from my [new] friends' town in the past, so they introduced me as their friend and this way Fernando agreed to get me across. I was told [that] people who had crossed with him walked a day less than those who walked with other guides. But the reason everybody liked Fernando was [that] he walked his clients to the point in the desert where they would board the trucks that would take them to Phoenix. Fernando only left our side when we were en route. That was why people trusted him so much and always sought his services. He took care of his people.

Drivers

Drivers transport border crossers from multiple points along the route. All known drivers in this study were men. Most drivers relied on their own vehicles to pick up border crossers at specific meeting points and then transported them to or from safe houses (locations where border crossers are housed while waiting for transportation or for payments to be processed), prearranged meeting points along a highway, shopping centers, train or bus stations, or to other locations from where border crossers could continue their journeys to their final destinations. Drivers were also known to work independently and offer their driving services to guides and coordinators. Some men reported having been approached randomly by people who, having just crossed the border, were seeking a ride to their destination in exchange for payment, although these cases were rare.

Most drivers in the sample were not residents of Arizona. They lived in other US states but drove to the Southwest whenever work opportunities arose. Many lived in neighboring states like California and New Mexico, but others would often drive from distant parts of the country for the potentially larger profits. Common places of residence, apart from California and Oregon along the US West Coast, were Alabama, Georgia, New York and Pennsylvania in the South and East Coast regions.

Often drivers had to pay upfront for all the related expenses (gas, meals and potential repairs). Some drivers were able to charge border crossers additional fees for extra services but as a general rule profits were solely dependent upon the number of people they were able to transport in their vehicles:

In Pennsylvania I met a guy who gave me a chance to transport people from Phoenix all the way back home for US$900. He gave me $500 for gas and expenses. Once I brought the people back home he paid me. The time when I was arrested was my second time driving people back east. I was going to get paid $800 for driving [11 people] this time, but I got caught.

Some drivers may also work as couriers, transporting money or other goods. Among those who work within Arizona, their collaborations may occasionally include the transportation or delivery of water and food to safe houses or rest stops along the migrant trail.

Some drivers, by virtue of the size of the smuggling group with whom they collaborate, reported driving rented, recent model vehicles. This tactic apparently reduced the risk of them being targeted during law enforcement operations, which often rely on racial profiling to target specific car styles or makes (Ortega Melendres et al. v. Arpaio 2013).[7] A coordinator explained:

We only send out people in new cars, and we make sure to send drivers that pass for white; this way they don't get stopped by the sheriff. The sheriffs are racist, they stop people because of how they look, so I always tell the drivers to look clean, to wear a nice shirt, and then we get them big, nice cars. That way nobody suspects they are driving people. But we always try to get drivers that look white. It is safer that way.

But for the majority of those who were arrested, renting newer vehicles was never an option. Most drivers, as a consequence of being undocumented, lacked driving licenses. They often used their own vehicles (which tended to be less reliable, older models prone to break down) or borrowed those of friends or family members. It was frequent to find people driving in pairs, especially in the case of long journeys, and profits were shared. Most arrests in fact involved this kind of arrangement. Arrests also resulted in the confiscation of vehicles by law enforcement. Multiple respondents also reported having been border crossers themselves who were approached by facilitators with the opportunity of reducing their fees in exchange for driving. Chapter 4 details these cases as forms of entry into the smuggling market.

Safe house staff

Border crossers often spend time at safe or drop houses while in transit to a destination or while waiting for pick-up. These locations may be private homes, or houses and facilities rented specifically for the purpose of temporarily accommodating those in transit. Some men and women participate in smuggling by housing border crossers for a few nights while awaiting transportation arrangements to their final destination. The main task of the safe house staff is to provide those in transit with meals and a place to sleep. Many women were reportedly employed at safe houses, being in charge of fixing meals and cleaning. Several people reported having been offered jobs as cooks or maids in exchange for a reduction of their fees.

Among the documented cases in this study, most facilitators in this category were people whose work schedules and living spaces allowed them to temporarily provide shelter. Most involved mothers who worked day shifts at fast food restaurants and elderly men and women who were unable to work outside of their home. Those hosted at safe houses while in transit often spoke of the treatment they received, referring to facilitators as kind and protective, and of being treated "like family" by ensuring that they had a place to rest and eat before they continued their journey. This was the case for two young men who referred to the woman who housed them "as a very nice lady who fed us dinner, set us up a clean place to sleep and, along with two other women, fixed us breakfast the next morning before the coyote stopped by to pick us up." Official documents also attested to the many times facilitators would provide those in transit with clean clothes, medication, and food and water for the rest of their journeys. One report described a raid into a safe house that resulted in the arrest of only one person: a young man who had crossed the border a couple of days earlier: "He was wearing warm pants and clean shoes; he looked rested and was watching television as he sat in the living room and waited for his ride to California." (Maricopa County v. De Jesus 2009, p. 2).

Whenever large numbers of migrants were housed at safe houses, men and women were often hired to provide services like cleaning, cooking and running errands. A police report documenting a raid described the arrest of 15 women and their children. The children were playing in the backyard while the women, relaxed and happy, were working at preparing a meal. Nobody appeared to have endured stress or violence. The person in charge of the house had avoided arrest, most likely unintentionally—she had gone on a grocery run for some missing ingredients.

Guards

While the human smuggling market is not inherently violent—a point further explored in Chapter 6—there was a tendency among some facilitators to employ males who could provide what was referred to as "security" or protection. The presence of guards seemed to be connected to the increase in police surveillance, but was also tied to the activities of *bajadores* (rip-off crews who often engage in home invasions and are known to kidnap border crossers from the locations where they are housed). Most guards are paid a weekly salary for their services, although others reported being paid a commission for each person staying in a safe house and whom they helped protect.

The presence of armed guards at safe houses was often interpreted in court documents as evidence of coercion or extortion. Guards, however, were often hired to create the illusion of protection in light of violent events. Furthermore, their presence was not always feared by border crossers, who instead considered them as an additional layer of protection offered by coyotes. One woman stated: "At the safe house where I stayed the guards were always good to me. I could get food, water and use the bathroom whenever I needed it, and I always felt safe."

Simultaneously, several facilitators reflected on the need for guards as enforcers as a result of the changing nature of the smuggling facilitator/border crosser dynamics. There were multiple reports of an increased tendency among border crossers to flee safe houses or to disappear without fulfilling their payments, in which case the presence of security guards could act as a (rather powerful) reminder of the clients' obligations. Still, the use of guards or of violence was rare. Guards rarely carried weapons. Excessive displays of security (such as look-outs, guards or the use of radios) were also considered dangerous as they generated unwanted attention. Despite the concerns of some smuggling facilitators, most agreements were fulfilled without the need for enforcement. One female coordinator spoke about her experience:

> One day two young men escaped the safe house without anybody noticing. They just walked out, and they still owed money. It was bad for everybody, because that is money we can't recover, and the people who help us may not be willing to work with us again. So sometimes I ask a couple of young men to come with me when I go to collect payments, so that people see [that] I am serious about getting paid. But I hardly ever have to do this, and besides it takes too much time to go look for people who owe you money. Sometimes you just take that as losses.

Like in other roles, guards were usually friends and family members hired for assistance. Yet a significant number of guards were also irregular border crossers in transit who reported being offered reduced fees or monetary compensation in exchange for their services:

> I did not have any money to pay my [smuggling fees] and so I had been working at the safe house for about three days [by the time the police arrived]. My job was to watch the [people] and to go to the grocery store to buy food to feed them. I do not have any immigration papers to live in the United States and so I was just working off my fees so that I could leave Phoenix. When police questioned me they asked if I thought [that] what I was doing was wrong [and] I replied that what I was doing is the way it is when you get smuggled.

Chapter 4 further explores the participation of irregular border crossers in transit in the facilitation of smuggling, and some of the implications of their involvement, including the occurrence of violent acts.

Coordinators

Coordinators are the first point of contact in the facilitation of a border crossing. They are primarily in charge of the logistical aspects of the journeys, their main role being to put facilitators and potential border crossers in contact with one another. Coordinators are also contacted by individuals looking for referrals for the transit of friends or family members. Often other facilitators reach out to coordinators looking for jobs.

Coordinators tend to be highly visible and recognized members of their community, known for their reliability and fairness in relation to facilitating border crossings. While they are active participants within the smuggling process, coordinators are typically perceived as third or neutral parties who can, in the event of abuses, mistreatment, unpaid fees or uncompensated services, act as mediators to assist all parties to reach an agreeable solution.

Coordinators often have long histories of residence within their neighborhoods, have extensive social circles and are highly aware of the resources available in their community. They have ample access to service providers and community stakeholders (such as pharmacists, nurses, law offices, attorneys, teachers and mechanics); and in the event of an unexpected crisis can assist in the provision of help. Coordinators also help with identifying vacant houses to rent as safe houses, obtain legal representation for people arrested as a result of smuggling and carry out multiple administrative tasks.

Another important role of coordinators also involves ensuring that facilitators get paid once smuggling fees have been received, and were at times paid a small commission for their services:

> Rosa Hernandez was my partner; we set up the safe house. She talked to the owner of the house, signed the rental contract, and maintained contact with almost all of the guards. We would receive people at the house and feed them and get their fees. She had asked for compensation, but she was always asked to wait. She had been working as a housekeeper, but work had been slow, she hadn't had as many hours and so she thought we could rely on smuggling while work got better to get by.

One important characteristic among coordinators involved the issue of income. Coordinators did not always receive monetary compensation for their services (that was particularly the case for women). Coordinator roles are considered privileged positions primarily because of the amount of social capital, leverage and recognition they generate. Hence coordinators performed a considerable amount of work and mobilized their circles in order to facilitate clients' transits, but they benefited mostly in non-monetary ways. Chapter 5 explores women's experiences in smuggling and the issue of social capital as income.

Helpers

Ayudantes are, in the majority, men in charge of performing basic, everyday tasks in support of coordinators. They transport cash, deliver equipment like radios or cell phones, drop off or recover vehicles, and pick up and deliver food or water. Their close contacts to a coordinator often meant benefiting from the coordinator's degree of social recognition and interaction in the community. Some of these helpers may eventually move on to perform other tasks, yet they primarily interacted with other facilitators, not with clients. One coordinator in this study spoke about a young teen who had assisted him as an *ayudante*:

That kid Honduras was a good kid. We took him right from the street, just like that. He came to us asking for a job, doing anything, he said. We put him [sic] to mop the rooms, to bring food for people, to get my lunch. He never complained, he never said no. Not like those other lazy bastards. In only a few weeks he was walking small groups. He's got all my trust, you know? He earned it. He's not like others who just come to see what they can get out of you. He wanted a job, an opportunity. And I am glad I gave it to him.

Financial services (cambiadores)

A fundamental element of smuggling involves the payment of smuggling fees to cover border crossing expenses. The tasks involved in financial transactions were often performed by women, rather than men. Women were more likely than men to be employed by companies in the formal economy, which required them to have valid bank accounts to process salary payments. Those involved at facilitating financial services—often referred to as *cambiadores*—verify deposits, make withdrawals and transfer fees. Typically, once a smuggling payment has been made via a money transfer, the person in transit notifies the facilitators. The facilitators then verify that the payment has been made and proceed to make a withdrawal.

Renato Serna, a 33-year-old US citizen, became involved in smuggling in an attempt to avoid a family feud from escalating. The investigation reports show Serna "and his wife [were] trying to move to get away from her family, because they [were] bad people"(Maricopa County v. Serna 2005). Given his citizenship status, he did not have a problem getting an identification card, which he used to cash money wires at a local store.

While Serna did benefit financially from his collaboration with his wife's relatives (he was paid between US$50 and US$100 for each money wire that he cashed), he was frequently forced to jump in to solve financial disputes among family members who had a hard time keeping their accounts straight; he was growing weary of his participation, but feared his wife's relatives would stop talking to her. Serna was portrayed in legal records as the financial mastermind of the organization, despite the fact that the only financial activity he was determined to conduct was the cashing of money wires. He was sentenced to a 14-month prison term and probation.

As other smuggling scholars have noted, successful journeys depend on the participation of multiple facilitators who perform specialized tasks (see Zhang 2007; Spener 2009a; Koser 2008). While the classification of labor outlined above describes the most representative roles found within human smuggling operations, it is by no means exhaustive. The adaptability and improvisation that characterize smuggling create multiple other activities or tasks that may not be explicitly discussed here. Facilitators may have to perform additional or different tasks at various times, especially if they are part of a small smuggling circle or provide services independently.

Conclusion

The narratives that cast smuggling groups as complex, highly organized and hierarchical, and smuggling facilitators as profit-driven, violent and exploitative, are challenged by the experiences and testimonies of those who participate in smuggling operations. The women and men interviewed for this project demonstrated limited interest in being part of large groups, valuing instead their independence and ability to work on their own terms and schedule. All lived rather ordinary lives, supporting families with the income generated from jobs in both the formal and informal economies.

Furthermore, the reflections of smuggling facilitators on the ways in which they organize and structure their activities challenged official characterizations of smuggling at multiple levels. There was, for example, no specific profile of smuggling facilitators; and labor and tasks were highly gendered, with some roles primarily involving men, such as driving, security and guidance, while highly visible and important roles like recruitment, logistics and financing were played by women. The reliance on security is by no means a synonym of violence, and rather serves as protection against the threat of kidnappings and law enforcement surveillance.

Smuggling facilitators are also highly independent, working alongside friends and family but not dependent upon any kind of central leadership, aside from the occasional effort of a coordinator or partner. Along these lines, smuggling is rather dependent on resources and connections. Some efforts may involve more people than others, but there was no evidence of criminal networks or transnational organizations of the kind described in official discourses participated in the market. Most journeys are the result of ad hoc collaborations among facilitators and, increasingly, the work of the very migrants and refugees they transport.

The provision of smuggling services does involve the crossing of international borders—yet the notion that smuggling facilitators operate transnationally obscures the fact that the irregular immigration status of most facilitators (as in the case of the men and women who facilitate extralegal border crossings in Maricopa County) constrains operations to the local sphere. This was particularly the case for women, who primarily worked within their own neighborhoods. It was more common for men to live in other US states, but they also faced the risk of being detained and charged with driving without legal authorization (unattainable due to their immigration status). While there is a transnational component to the operation of smuggling, efforts are not necessarily transnationally organized. Often the immigration status of those participating in the facilitation of border crossings limited their ability to operate beyond their local communities and borders. At the same time, it is also true that smuggling is dependent on the nature of global communications and their increased affordability (yet it should not be interpreted as an indicator of complex technological abilities, as some scholars have argued).

Profits made by facilitators were rather small; the average compensation allowed men or women merely to supplement their salaries. The seasonal nature of smuggling also meant that the activity could not be relied upon as a permanent form of income. Participation in smuggling was always a sporadic, seasonal activity, providing an occasional source of income.

The overview of the smuggling market provided in this chapter has described its constitution and organization. While the state constantly refers to smuggling networks as dominated by powerful criminal interests, the findings reveal the market to be comprised of independent facilitators who assist one another to cross borders extralegally on a sporadic basis, and without criminal intentions. The organization of the smuggling market highlights its community-based nature and how it provides income-generating opportunities for the poor. Rather than constituting a conspiratorial effort to overthrow state controls, participation in smuggling can be seen as a concerted effort among families and friends to generate supplementary resources within a community that is unlikely to ascend socially or economically. The temporary profits generated by participation in the smuggling market are immediately recycled into the local economy and are not likely to contribute to the creation of wealth among those who participate.

Notes

1 US Immigration Service.
2 With the exception of five who held citizenship or residence permits, the other 61 lacked authorization to legally reside in the US.
3 Zhang refers to this property as the "dyadic model of smuggling."
4 For a discussion on the facilitation of crossings for children or pregnant women by female facilitators, refer to Chapter 5.
5 "The other side," figuratively referring to the US.
6 Irregular migrants.
7 Along with undocumented residents, US-born citizens of Latino origin were also identified in the sample. While it appears the local smuggling market is almost entirely run by non-white facilitators, the occasional presence of non-Latino participants may be yet another indicator of the open membership of some of the smuggling groups. During the data collection process, the cases of a white female and an Asian male were identified – the female, a US citizen, was sentenced to a probation term, while charges against the Asian male were dropped. Since human smuggling enforcement relies heavily on perceptions of race and ethnic origin, non-Latino participation in the Arizona market may be taking place but continue undetected, although this assumption is largely speculative. Non-Latinos may be able to operate as they are more likely to avoid detection and arrest, primarily on the basis of their physical appearance. Given that they are not perceived as likely to be associated in smuggling, there is less chance they will be stopped by law enforcement under the suspicion of being involved in the transportation of undocumented immigrants. The size of the sample, however, did not allow for the determination of the frequency of these collaborations.

4 "I am not a pollero"

Smugglers on smuggling

> This was your last little trip, pollero. I am not a pollero, said Chucho. Ha! Right. I have seen you crossing people, the rancher said, and I caught you in the act. No. It is not the act what I deny. But I am not a pollero.
>
> (Yuri Herrera 2010, *Señales que precederán al fin del mundo* [*Signs that will precede the end of the world*])

Rayo—or John Doe 46, according to his court indictment—is a medium-build, tall man with black, wavy hair. Every day at 7:30am, he arrives at this run-down, two-story hotel in Phoenix, and sits in the small, crowded room that serves him as an office. In it there is a table covered with papers—receipts of wire transfers, semi-torn business cards, pieces of paper covered with what appear to be cell-phone numbers—and a small safety box that does not lock, in which he keeps a ledger. There are also a few old cell phones, scratched and with cracked screens – signs that they get used, and dropped, too often. The cell phones are beeping. Rayo has messages or missed calls that he must tend to but which he tries to ignore. First he must call Güera, his girlfriend, who supports herself by selling fresh juice and sandwiches to the employees of businesses in this predominantly migrant neighborhood in Phoenix. Rayo has to ask her to accompany him to pick up a wire transfer from a man in Indiana who has just finished paying his smuggling fee. Güera, a US citizen by birth, is the only one with a valid passport in this small group of friends who work as "*pasando gente,*" or "crossing people."

Unable to further ignore the cell phones, Rayo tells himself "I will call her later and ask her," pulling up a chair and finally sitting down to listen to his messages. Here in Phoenix, Trini needs a call back; she has not been paid for the two young men she referred to Rayo, and her rent is now due. Roman is asking how many cars he should get this week and for how many people. One of the men Rayo has asked to drive people to Los Angeles is running late, and he needs money for gas. Rayo curses under his breath, "This driver must be an idiot . . . a driver who runs out of gas . . . " and starts making calls.

The stories of Rayo, Güera and their friends reflect some of the everyday dynamics surrounding the provision of extralegal border crossings in Arizona—an occupation that has become, despite its illicit nature, a labor and income-generating strategy along the routes of the migrant trail; one that is performed alongside full- or part-time jobs—and in some cases, as a primary source of income.

In this chapter, I provide further evidence of how the lack of empirical data on smuggling has led us to recognize smuggling only partially as a socially embedded, collective process aimed at overcoming marginalization. Efforts to map smuggling in terms of linearity, networks and structure have masked the individual experiences of the actors involved, while the emphasis on the smuggler as a self-standing character in the mythology of borders has obscured the degree of collaboration—and conflict—among facilitators themselves, along with their clients. This last aspect is of particular importance, given that significant numbers of those arrested for smuggling offenses are in fact migrants or refugees in transit, recruited to perform smuggling tasks, and who most often become targets of violence or criminalization efforts (Ahmad 2011; Weber and Grewcock 2011).

This chapter documents facilitators' experiences in human smuggling—their paths and rationale to participation, the challenges they face and eventually the factors leading to their exit from the market. I once again rely on both legal records and facilitators' own statements to map the relationships and processes that characterize their participation in smuggling. By continuing to explore the role of community, solidarity, structural inequality and personal experiences present in the smuggling process, the testimonies highlight the wide range of motives behind such participation, which often go beyond the desire for financial profit, and are often dependent on enforcement, family pressure or altruistic goals. The chapter continues to show how facilitators challenge common perceptions of smuggling as profit-driven, as being hierarchical in nature or as dependent on domination, territories or turf, instead emphasizing its viability as a legitimate and worthwhile form of labor.

The dignifying power of labor and the day-to-day challenges associated with its social nature are two of the primary themes to emerge from facilitators' understandings of their participation in smuggling. The search for respect within marginalized communities, and the need to re-establish a sense of dignity in the context of widespread unemployment, the terror inflicted by immigration raids, family separations and the racial discrimination and exclusion pervasive in Arizona also emerge as frequent topics. Additionally, the role of solidarity and assistance among equals remains important, understood as the sharing of resources and opportunities, allowing others to reduce the impact of forms of inequality (ranging from the lack of access to health care for low-income or women-headed households to the absence of viable employment options for members of immigrant families). Lastly, there is a constant effort among facilitators to rewrite the rhetoric of their actions as criminal, by placing their actions in opposition to the language of organized crime, border violence and victimization, instead asserting their right to survive in an environment hostile to their efforts at building a better life. In this sense, smuggling has emerged as a form of labor through which people along the border "defend themselves against attempts by the state or the market to exert control over their labor and productive capacities" (Vélez-Ibáñez 1996, 137).

This chapter thus explores Maricopa County's human smuggling facilitators' experiences at work.

"Becoming" a coyote: entry into smuggling

There are no formal mechanisms or processes leading to an individual's participation in smuggling operations. Entry into smuggling is largely fortuitous (Zhang 2007, 2009): a combination of social interactions and connections and having access to specific resources.

Most smuggling facilitators in this sample began their participation in smuggling through kin and kith relations, working alongside family members or very close friends who had been in turn introduced by other close friends or family (Chin 1999; Zhang 2007; Spener 2009a; van Liempt 2007). Participation was most often the result of immediate access to other groups of facilitators or resources that could be called upon during a smuggling operation—resources that ranged from a running vehicle to acquaintances along the border; from official forms of identification like driving licenses or border crossing cards to having access to real estate or a stable housing situation, etc. There was no evidence that facilitators were connected to other criminal organizations or involved in any other kind of criminalized activity. In most cases, resources were individually owned.

Other facilitators reported having been recruited during their own journeys as undocumented immigrants. They were offered to drive a vehicle, to clean a safe house or to cook in exchange for reduced fees. In addition to receiving a discount on their smuggling expenses, many of them reported having been compensated financially for their services.

Immigration law enforcement and border controls have also allowed for the emergence of a very specific kind of smuggling facilitator—those deported as a result of immigration raids or employment verification operations who become involved in smuggling as the means to pay off their fees to return home. (The majority of men facing felony convictions in Maricopa County for their involvement in smuggling that were identified as part of this project were in fact border crossers trying to re-enter the country following their deportation, and not "career smugglers" per se.) Gender also plays a role in smuggling involvement, with women facing gender-specific challenges.[1] Lastly, multiple respondents also reported entering smuggling on the basis of their own entrepreneurial drive and desire for income-generating opportunities. Regardless of the road taken, happenstance (echoing Zhang 2008, 29) appears to be a recurrent element of participation in smuggling, as the following testimonies can attest.

Relatives and friends

For most facilitators, their introduction into smuggling came via their immediate social contacts. They had friends or family members who were already involved in smuggling or who were in contact with individuals providing smuggling services. Margot, who worked occasionally collecting smuggling fees, explained:

My cousin lived in Mexico. She and her husband worked in Sonora with a group that would send people to Arizona, and so she asked me to help her collect money from people who were being brought across. The fees would go into my bank account, and then I would receive US$50 for every deposit. Sometimes she would ask me to bring the money down to the border, and she would also pay me for that.

Multiple responses identified connections initiated by friends as a common entry point into smuggling. In other words, acquaintances become important sources of information on jobs and tips for potential income-generating opportunities (O'Leary and Sanchez 2011), including those in the underground economy like smuggling. Victor Castillo, for instance, had lost his job at the construction company where he had worked for three consecutive years. One of his former coworkers approached him and invited him to assist a group of friends who were smuggling small groups of migrants. His wife shared the family's experience:

One of Victor's coworkers knew he was unemployed and that he had been looking for work after he got laid off. He also knew we had two children to support. So he said he could help and offered Victor a job. My husband was taking food and water to the people at the safe house. His friend was paying him $300 per week for his help. There were also times when I would take messages and cash wire transfers, and I would also get paid for that.

Narratives of solidarity among friends and coworkers as paths into smuggling of the kind described by Victor Castillo's wife were very common. In fact, invitations to collaborate in smuggling were frequently extended to those who were perceived as in critical financial need, regardless of the existence of blood or friendship ties. Jose Emilio crossed the border through the desert "without the use of a guide or coyote, using the sun as a guide and walking for 3 days" (Maricopa County v. Medina Meraz 2009). Police reports state Emilio arrived at Phoenix's homeless shelter where he "slept and bathed while he looked for work." A couple of days later at a nearby convenience store Emilio ran into an old acquaintance who occasionally collaborated in smuggling activities as a driver. Emilio explained to him he had just crossed the border back into the US and was in need of a job, and so his friend invited him to move in with his family. For the next three days, Emilio "stayed in the backyard, eating and sleeping in a car and only going into the house occasionally to use the restroom; he stayed outside out of respect for his friend, who had a wife and daughters" (Maricopa County v. Medina-Meraz 2009). Emilio repaired his friend's car and he was paid a few hundred dollars in cash (US$400).

What Emilio ignored was that his friend had already been identified by police as an active smuggling facilitator and, during a nighttime operation, a SWAT (special weapons and tactics) team irrupted at his home. Emilio—and not his friend—was arrested and charged with collaborating with a smuggling group, his money confiscated as evidence. While the charges were ultimately dropped, Emilio was eventually deported and his earnings were never returned to him.

Entrepreneurship

As Zhang identified in his research on Chinese human smuggling, entrepreneurial inclination, primarily evident in an individual's self-organization of an income-generating opportunity (in the legal and underground economies), was common in smuggling. Identifying opportunities to provide specific services involving extralegal border crossings provided some of the respondents with the ability to generate an income, often despite their lack of employment authorization. A number of facilitators also were or had been businesses owners at some point in their lives—entrepreneurial pasts were quite common among women—what further facilitated their ability to conduct business.

Natalie Martinez was a 49-year-old single mother of two teenage sons. For most of her time in the US (where she had arrived as a 19-year-old from Mexico following the end of an abusive relationship), she had relied on self-employment to support her family due to her lack of employment authorization. For many years, she worked selling food out of a truck that she drove to local construction sites during the week. But after the decline of the construction industry in Maricopa County, business became scarce. Natalie sold the truck, obtained a hairdressing license and went to work at a beauty salon as a stylist. It was there where she met two brothers, Omar and Jose Luis Ramos, who frequently talked about their involvement in smuggling. Natalie approached the brothers about the possibility of helping them:

> They knew me from the salon. They would come and I would hear them talk about their business. One day I just approached them and told them I knew a lot of people from my other job, that I could help them get clients. That was how I started working with them. People who needed to cross would just call me on my phone, and then I would check with Jose Luis and see if there was room for someone in a car, and if he said yes I could then call the person back with a price quote.

Natalie had no prior contacts or experience in smuggling. When she first entered the US, she did it on a visa, and did not have to rely on smuggling facilitators. She was aware, from the media and her clients, about the work of coyotes. But until she approached the Ramos brothers she had never envisioned herself providing any services related to border crossings. She primarily relied on her business savvy and her ability to communicate and create rapport with potential clients— skills she displayed in her work as a smuggling coordinator.

Financing one's own journey

A considerable number of respondents entered smuggling in an attempt to finance their own cross-border journeys. This fact is significant as it further challenges the perception of human smuggling groups as tightly knit operations open to a select few. On the other hand, the overrepresentation of people seeking to self-fund their border crossing among those convicted for human smuggling raises concerns about facilitators' reliance on those who are least able to afford smuggling fees as cannon fodder, while simultaneously avoiding detection and arrest.

Legal case files and personal accounts reflect how men and women seeking to cross the border, but who lack the financial resources or social capital needed to do so, approach smuggling facilitators with the hope of negotiating lower fees or travel in exchange for work. A court affidavit summarizes the experience of one such man:

> Martinez received a call from an unidentified male, who narrated [that] his mother was sick and that [he] needed to travel to Oregon, where he was certain he would be able to secure employment. Martinez quoted the ongoing price of $2200 for full transportation. The unidentified male replied [that] he was unable to pay the fee at that point and lost his composure. Martinez asked the unidentified male if he had any skills. He replied [that] he could do anything, but that most of his life he had worked the fields. Martinez gave the unidentified male the number to her niece in Nogales, and told him to call her. Martinez assured him [that] her niece (also involved in smuggling) would be able to employ him so that he could save up and finance his trip.
>
> (Maricopa County v. Martinez-Ponce, 2007, Affidavit)

There were also instances where the need for help emerged suddenly during a journey,[2] border crossers becoming unexpectedly involved in facilitating their own transits. Horacio Felix, for example, had agreed to pay US$2500 for his entire journey. As he waited in a safe house in Phoenix for the transportation that would take him to San Jose, California, a smuggling facilitator entered the house and asked if anybody in the group knew how to drive. Felix raised his hand. He accepted an offer to have his fee reduced by US$500 in exchange for his driving services. Javier Alvarado's experience was similar:

> I was taken to a safe house in Phoenix, where there were 38 other people. I had been charged $2500 to come to the United States, and I came to an agreement with the coyotes that my family would pay the coyote in Mexico. The day of my arrest, one of the coyotes asked our group [of migrants] if anyone could drive, and I raised my hand and I said I could. The coyote offered to reduce my fee to $2000 if I drove one of the vans transporting people.

Facing staffing shortages, large numbers of customers to transport or the unavailability of specific resources (in this sample, vehicles or drivers), facilitators extend opportunities for customers to assist them in their tasks. While in this study the majority of these cases involved men asked to provide driving services, many others reported working at safe houses cooking, cleaning or acting as guards. Such was the case of Audias Orozco, who was trying to find a way to travel to California but lacked the funds to cover the cost of the final leg of his journey (US$500). He spoke to his smuggling facilitator, who told him he could work at the safe house to pay off his fees. Orozco agreed. Orozco had been working for 15 days cooking and running errands at the time police raided the safe house (Maricopa County v. Orozco-Izazaga 2009, 8).

Surveillance reports describe how Orozco would leave the house at least once a day and return pushing a supermarket cart carrying food for those staying at the house. The reports further suggest that the migrants staying at the house were aware of Orozco's agreement with the smuggling facilitators, as they often tried to advocate on Orozco's behalf in court by stating, "He was one of us"—just another client working off his fees. Orozco's actions toward the other migrants were never violent, yet his participation in smuggling was constructed in police reports as a "threat to the Phoenix community" and his sentencing recommendation called for "stiff penalties that send a message to smugglers out there that this kind of behavior will not be tolerated in Maricopa County" (Maricopa County v. Orozco Izazaga 2009, presentence report).

A one-time collaboration has the potential of turning into an ongoing partnership between an immigrant and his or her smuggling facilitator. Sporadic contacts may evolve into long-term business relationships that are valued by migrants as occasional opportunities to supplement their incomes. During a visit to Phoenix, Martin Cruz received a call from an acquaintance for whom he had transported a small group of immigrants a few years back. The caller asked Cruz if he was interested in driving 12 passengers back to Tennessee, where he now lived. Each one of the passengers would pay Cruz US$100 for his services. Cruz saw the opportunity to make some extra cash and accepted the offer (Maricopa County v. Cruz-Rosette 2009). He picked up his passengers at a busy intersection in a predominantly migrant neighborhood in Phoenix and was already on his way to Tennessee when he was pulled over by an officer conducting random plate checks during one of the sheriff's office "crime suppression operations."

The prior cases exemplify how border crossers themselves enter smuggling in an attempt to reduce their fees or eliminate considerable portions of debt. These arrangements are particularly beneficial to smuggling groups, who deflect risk onto their clients, and can frequently avoid arrest. Working off fees has become an acceptable—if ethically questionable—compromise in the relationship between facilitator and client, amid increased staffing shortages in the smuggling game. This change, however, increases the vulnerability of the client, the risks and implications emerging from an arrest transferred to a (often unsuspecting) migrant who may simply be trying to reduce the impact of loans and long-term debt.

"I just wanted to make them happy": the motives

Zhang (2008) and Spener (2009b) report that snakeheads and coyotes participate in smuggling mostly as a way to improve their living conditions, and in response to financial need. Both authors would argue that involvement in the large majority of cases is a carefully calculated decision given its potential to provide relatively reasonable profits while facing relatively low risks.

In this project there was, however, no single, unique motive leading to an individual's participation in smuggling. Instead, participation is borne of a combination of factors that evince smuggling's role as a mechanism to overcome structural limitations to social mobility through a reliance on community ties.

For the majority of facilitators, smuggling constitutes a path to increased social capital and recognition. Many were adamant that their participation contributes to the wellbeing of others. The recognition of similar experiences to their own among their clients was a constant theme in the interviews, as was an awareness of the impact current immigration control and enforcement policies have on decisions to become a facilitator.

Among respondents, there was also an ethical element to their participation—namely the assistance provided to people who, as facilitators or clients, would otherwise face high levels of risk and vulnerability. Furthermore, all of the facilitators shared an understanding of smuggling as a legitimate form of labor. Facilitators have in this sense developed a code of values and expectations (Galemba 2012a, 2012b) that defines their relationships not only with their clients, but also with each other.

For those who cited financial need as a reason, the lack of employment options in the formal economy due to their immigration status was the reason most frequently cited for smuggling involvement.

Isai Zuniga had not had a steady job for about a year by the time he became involved in human smuggling. He had managed to support himself by working occasionally as a gardener and carpenter, but without a job permit his employment stability was limited, if existent at all. A friend concerned about his financial situation referred him to his contacts in smuggling. Through his participation, Zuniga was for the first time able to save some money. And so after conducting several trips for his friends' group (he was working as a driver), he managed to save enough money to afford the rental deposit for a house. His girlfriend, a US citizen, was pregnant with his first child and the family had for a long time needed a place to live:

> I was a driver. I would pick up *indocumentados* in Naco and then drive them to a house in Phoenix, but I didn't have anything [else] to do with them. I got paid $150 per person I dropped off at the [safe] house. I did ten or fifteen trips for what I can remember, and then I got caught. [I participated in smuggling] because I needed money, I did not have a steady job and I am *ilegal.* But most importantly, my girlfriend was going to have a baby and she needed a place to stay.
>
> (Maricopa County v. Zuniga 2007, 2)

Despite being aware of the circumstances that limited Zuniga's ability to become gainfully employed, the presentence investigator working on his case characterized him as "an individual willing to risk the lives of others to meet his own needs, committing the [present] offenses [. . .] for pure financial greed" (Maricopa County v. Zuniga 2007, 3). The report does not mention his efforts to provide housing for his growing family.

Immigration enforcement also plays a role in respondents' decisions to become involved in smuggling. During the entire Obama administration, there has been a significant increase in the number of deportations—one that in fact has far exceeded the number seen under the administration of former President George W. Bush Junior, whose immigration enforcement practices were for many years criticized for their extreme nature (Gonzalez-Barrera and Lopez 2013; US Immigration and Customs Enforcement 2013).

These immigration enforcement efforts had a considerable impact on the make-up of the border crossing population. A report containing the testimonies of over 1000 extralegal border crossers produced by the Binational Migration Institute (BMI) revealed that half of those surveyed had at least one family member who was a US citizen, and that one in four had a US-born child (Martinez et al. 2013, 11). The changing face of deportees—who traditionally had been perceived as single males with no ties in the US—is also reflected among those involved in smuggling. In this sample, a significant number of men arrested during immigration raids while trying to return home to their families were involved in the facilitation of smuggling services. David Rojas worked for a smuggling organization he joined after several failed attempts to cross the border on his own:

> In January I tried to come back from Mexico to Colorado, where I used to live before I was deported after a raid at work. In Phoenix I was taken to a drop house and I was supposed to stay there until I could pay my fee, but after some days it was just evident that I had no [way of getting the money], so I begged the coyotes to let me go and they did. I kept trying [to come back], but by then it was already March, and I hadn't had any luck at crossing. I was desperate. So this man saw me and approached me at the bus station in Naco and asked me if I wanted to make some money and get back into the States. [He said] I had to recruit other people for him at the bus station. I got him 30 people and I got paid $200 for my work. Since he saw I was good at getting people the man asked me to work with him.
>
> (Maricopa County v. Zuniga 2007, 2–3)

The presentence report submitted to the court in Rojas' case frames his actions as those of "a trusted gang member chosen to recruit business, drive and guide illegal aliens across the border." Not only are these statements examples of the court system's limited understanding of smuggling operations, by describing Rojas' actions as those of a gang member, but they also fail to grasp the social meaning of his experience.

Court documents are correct in describing Rojas' activities as "integral [. . .] to [. . .] the operation's success," although the characterization of his actions as "having a negative impact upon the community, since his participation was motivated by his need to financially further himself" is in itself questionable. The evidence presented in court established Rojas worked for or collaborated with the human smuggling groups over several months, but he was never paid more than US$200 per crossing, which is in line with what other guides reported as the average payment for their group-crossing services (an amount that also attests to smuggling's low returns). Rojas was eventually found guilty of human smuggling and was sentenced to two and a half years in prison.

Armando Jara's construction job had been another casualty in the collapse of the local Arizona housing market. After being laid off, he had not been able to secure a job in months. During the 13 years he had lived in the country as an undocumented immigrant, he had been able to work in construction, and he had never come into contact with police, not even for a traffic violation. He was embarrassed to admit he was forced to apply for welfare so that he could feed his children—who were US citizens—and was receiving a few hundred dollars every month on food stamps, but that was not enough to support his family. An acquaintance asked him if he would be willing to drive a few migrants into Phoenix for money.

> My partner and I were going to be paid $3000 for driving the people into Phoenix. I did it because I had not had a job for over 8 months. I have five children, and my wife gets food stamps but that was not enough. I was just supposed to drive the four people into Phoenix and once we got there I was going to get a call and I was going to be told where to take them.
>
> (Maricopa County v. Jara-Montelano 2009)

Jara was driving a Jeep when a police officer began to follow him. When he saw the vehicle, Jara became nervous and sped away, driving into a gas station nearby, from where his passengers jumped the vehicle and escaped. He stood by the Jeep and waited for the officer to arrest him—none of his passengers (which included a pregnant woman) were found.

Jara was charged with human smuggling but was released to immigration authorities before his case was heard in court and was deported almost immediately. His smuggling case not settled, an arrest order was immediately issued. Since he was his family's sole provider, he faced the decision of returning to the US to support his children or to stay in Mexico. He chose to come back to his family, but was arrested by the US Border Patrol as he re-entered the country illegally as the arrest order on his pending case for human smuggling emerged. Jara was sent to Maricopa County to face the charges. He spent three months in state custody while his case was heard in court and was sentenced to a two-year probation term. However, he was also expected to be released to immigration authorities to face additional charges at the federal level for illegal re-entry.[3]

Facilitators also explain their involvement in smuggling as fueled by their desire to help other immigrants like themselves. That is the case of men like Rafael Sanchez, who admitted to law enforcement officers his role as driver of a smuggling operation when stopped along a highway for a traffic violation. Just like other facilitators, Sanchez entered smuggling after he was unable to find any other form of employment for months. But he ultimately decided to become a driver as a way of paying back the favors others had done for him when he first crossed the border:

I know how tough the crossing is for a migrant and his family. Everybody suffers. I was very fortunate, because when I crossed, I had a very good experience, and that was because good people helped me along the way: the coyote; the first person to give me a job, and the one who let me stay in his home while I got on my feet. That is why I decided to do this. I know I was getting paid but in a way I am just paying forward what others did for me. I just wanted to make people happy.

(Maricopa County v. Sanchez-Reyes 2009a, 2009b)

Celso Chavez also referred to his experience in smuggling as a way to assist others. His friend and codefendant, Abraham Aguilar, had six children and was having a hard time providing for them. Chavez, a gardener, was approached by an acquaintance and asked if he would transport 10 undocumented immigrants from Phoenix to Los Angeles for US$600. He thought this would be an opportunity to earn some money while also helping Aguilar and, against his wife's advice, he invited his friend to join him in the trip and split the profits. Chavez's goal was to help his friend and the migrants they transported:

I agreed to transport the people to California, but not just for the money. They are travelers, we all are travelers, and they needed help to reach their destination. When I first came to the US as an *ilegal* someone was kind enough to give me [a job] so that I could travel to California to work and support my family. I regret my actions—my wife told me this was risky, and she told me not to do it—but I have always been law abiding, and I make an honest living. I clean up yards and I make about $1500 per month. That is how I support my family.

(Maricopa County v. Nazario-Chavez 2006)

While financial motives are initially disclosed as the cause leading most smuggling facilitators to participate in smuggling, narratives consistently point at how community members help each other to support their families and maintain a sense of dignity in poverty. The solidarity and cooperation that takes place among low-income, working class immigrants are concepts that run counter to the anti-immigrant, vilifying discourse that dominates the global rhetoric of migration and smuggling.

At the same time, this view of collaboration and mutual support must not be romanticized. If anything, the existence of underground economies among the poor reveals at many levels the desperate conditions they face—to the point that risky actions like the ones some facilitators conduct in smuggling are seen as the only option to secure one's family's subsistence. And yet, as these narratives have shown, an individual's participation in smuggling is primarily the result of heartfelt offers of help and constitutes a demonstration of solidarity that eventually allows for the survival of entire migrant families and their children.

Self-perceptions of participation

When Zulema Martinez was questioned about her involvement in smuggling, she stated she "honestly believed" she was doing no wrong. For several years she had worked assisting an unknown number of immigrants and their families by putting them in contact with a group of drivers who in turn provided border crossing and transportation services. She also remarked during her in-court interrogation that many of those she had assisted were her friends and relatives. "I paid so that I could bring some of them over. I paid so that my relatives could come. I don't think I did anything wrong by doing that."

Facilitators' perceptions of their roles as providers of extralegal border crossings are important elements to consider within an analysis of their overall experience of smuggling. Hardly any smuggling facilitator explained his or her involvement in extralegal crossings only in terms of financial profit. Their narratives instead reveal a more complex process, characterized by an honest concern for the wellbeing of others, in part a result of their own experiences as irregular immigrants, the challenges in seeking to provide for their families and their attempts to rejoin their families after being the target of enforcement. Most of the testimonies in this study reflected the ethical dimensions of their collaborations as facilitators of extralegal border crossings.

The narratives in this sample suggest smuggling facilitators considered their participation as constituting an opportunity to help others while improving their own social status. Sensing they could effectively help others perceived as vulnerable or in need helped facilitators designate their actions as positive and benevolent. A phone call transcript between two collaborating parties further attests to this perception: "I think I do something good for people. I help them come here, to be with their families, with their children. I think that's [the importance of] what we do" (Maricopa County v. Robaina 2006).

Smuggling is often perceived as being a central factor in the reunification of families who would otherwise face long physical separations as a result of immigration law. Through their actions, smuggling facilitators give families the opportunity to be together—reunions that would be delayed or even denied by current immigration processes and legislation.

Yet despite their awareness of the work that they conduct on behalf of other border crossers and migrants, facilitators often refuse to be identified as coyotes. Sitting in Rayo's small office, I overheard his conversation with a potential client:

Client: So you are Mr Rayo, right? I was told to call you.
Rayo: I go by many names, ma'am.
Client: Well, they just said you were a *pollero* and just to call you. That you would help us with what we needed.

Rayo was not amused by the woman's response. After a moment of silence, he sternly replied: "I go by many names, ma'am. Rayo, Guero, Chacho. Just use the name they gave you. I have a name. Don't call me a *pollero.*"

Rayo's conscious effort to establish a personal identity reflects his understanding of his participation in smuggling: that he is a man providing a legitimate service. He refused to be identified simply as a *pollero* or coyote, despite the fact that he was facilitating extralegal border crossings for a fee.

In the course of my interactions with the men and women involved in smuggling, I rarely perceived any attempts to make their roles appear professional; instead, every time they sought to be perceived as reliable, kind and respectful of people's lives. Facilitators made every effort to establish their specific contributions as meaningful to those who relied on their services and as valuable to their peers. None of them ever claimed membership to a specific group or family, to be central to the success of a specific group or to possess any kind of expertise. Rather, their statements reflected the ways in which their participation had allowed them to improve the lives of their families, and to establish—or, for many, regain—a sense of pride and dignity.

Perhaps it is facilitators' perception of the services they provide as only partial or segmented portions of a border crossing that prevents them from seeing their role as fully professional. This designation appeared to be left for what, in this sample, was seen as the idealized coyote—the smuggler working on his own, defying all limitations and delivering his clients from all evils. Not a single respondent in this sample was comfortable with identifying his or her actions as those of a coyote. Smuggling participants were adamant to affirm the limits of their participation in smuggling, refusing to identify their participation as a career, profession or even a full-time occupation. As seen in the following statement of Torres Alvarado to the court, facilitators often highlighted the fact that they held other jobs and that they should not be defined solely by their participation in smuggling:

> I am sorry for what I did. I did it because it seemed like an easy way to make some money so that I could send some home. But this is not my profession. I am an electrician and work construction. I am not a coyote.
>
> (Maricopa County v. Torres-Alvarado, 2009)

Most respondents did not consider any part of their involvement in smuggling to be deviant or criminal. They perceived the provision of these services as benevolent acts conducted on behalf of friends and family. In a letter to the court, the sister of a man accused of driving a car full of irregular migrants in transit similarly attempted to contextualize her brother's involvement in smuggling, while condemning the court's decision to convict him:

> He has 2 young children ([aged] 4 and 8) and his wife who are waiting for him here with us. We know you found him guilty. But guilty of what? Of looking out for his children because there are no jobs here? Guilty of taking on the responsibility to drive that van so that he could use the money to support his children? It is not fair that my brother has to pay, but only you know what his sentence should be because we cannot go to the Other Side where you are. He is desperate to [see] his kids and wife and how can he if he is in [detention] for no reason?

The prevalence of irregular migrants trying to self-finance their border crossings among those charged and convicted with human smuggling also reveals that the enforcement strategies adopted by local law enforcement agencies to combat extralegal border crossings has had minimal impact on stopping those seeking to cross the border extralegally, or on dismantling smuggling groups. Instead, enforcement has encouraged facilitators to find ways to ameliorate the impact of enforcement, and for those seeking to cross the border to undertake higher levels of risk.

The challenges of the smuggling market

Smuggling facilitators perceive their work as a mechanism to develop social recognition and status among the members of their social groups. Their work, however, is not exempt from challenges or frustrations, and while the market of smuggling is not inherently violent, conflict can arise among facilitators. Failed accounting methods, law enforcement pressures, detection and the everyday stresses of family life often impact a facilitator's ability to collaborate effectively with other facilitators.

Family interactions and conflict

Reports of conflict among smuggling groups were virtually non-existent in the sample (primarily in an effort to avoid unwanted attention from outsiders—including police). When present, conflict seems to take place within a group or family of facilitators, although it is typically solved (or, rather, tolerated) internally. Conflicts in smuggling arise primarily as a result and in the context of everyday interactions among facilitators, many of whom are also family members. In that sense, arguments are common among people who maintain not only business but also personal ties.

The majority of references to conflict in this sample involve family disagreements over how to run the business; failed romantic relationships among facilitators; or arguments between parents and their children, siblings or couples. Despite the prevalence of familial conflict, most smuggling facilitators are able to maintain their collaboration in smuggling without much distraction or delays. That does not mean these events do not cause frustration, as the following testimony from a smuggling facilitator suggests:

> Oh let me tell you . . . I brought my brother over because back home he had nothing to do; he was not going to school, he did not even have a girlfriend the son of a bitch and he would tell my mom that "he was bored." "I'm bored, I'm bored, I'm bored." It was freaking ridiculous. And so we thought: well, if the jackass is so bored, bring him over! Let's teach him who works so that he could buy those shoes he wears! And so we got him across and all the way here into [Phoenix]. And what did he do? Nothing. We would talk to him, bring him along to follow loads, tell him about the importance of talking to people straight, of treating customers well, of not letting them down, of being good to people, of always delivering. Because that is how we are: what you see is what you get, you know. And what did he do? Nothing. This new generation takes everything for granted, and they want to come and then take over a business it has taken you years to build. So we just sent him back. He can be bored down there the same way he was here.
> (Marquez, G. 2008. Personal Interview, Phoenix, Arizona)

Conflict in smuggling has a regulatory function. It serves as a mechanism to enforce agreements and exert discipline, and to create informal mechanisms for enforcement among facilitators. However, few incidents lead to physical violence, as threats are used as the primary form of enforcement. While smuggling facilitators avoid engaging in violent acts—after all, their role is to ensure a successful, safe journey—the presence of violence in smuggling of the kind exerted against border crossers cannot be denied. Chapter 6 will further explore the conditions that have allowed for the emergence of violent acts that primarily target migrants in transit.

Financial mishaps

Disagreements also arise from failed financial deals. Some facilitators are not very skilled at performing mathematical calculations, and reports of losses due to faulty accounting are common. However, despite the large amounts of cash that are handled, only one report of mishandling of funds by facilitators appeared in the sample.

There is an expectation that payments for services provided will be handled timely and responsibly, and that the coordinators will do their job to ensure everybody is paid. However, payments do get delayed frequently, leading to anger and even threats of no further collaboration. These conflicts are usually temporary and never impact operations in the long term. Even when serious disagreements or losses take place, facilitators get over their differences, continue collaborating with each other and reach out to fellow facilitators in time of need. Some relationships may be damaged, but people seem to work out their issues:

> Well, my husband used to work for Jose Luis. But they got into this fight because my husband—my ex, really—had some money that he was supposed to send back to the people in Mexico, and instead he went and spent it all at the casino. Jose Luis was pissed, he was so mad . . . and so they stopped talking to each other. Jose Luis had to pay the money out of his own pocket. But they still talk because they have known each other for years.

Competition

Competition did not seem to be a concern among the individuals and groups whose cases were analyzed. Most facilitators worked independently and did not seem to have exclusive ties to a single group, and instead collaborated freely with other individual providers like themselves. When a specific facilitator is unable to assist, the business is referred to another facilitator who may be available at the time. In return, the other facilitator may pay back with a future referral, or by sharing resources like drivers, walkers, money carriers, vehicles, etc. This collaboration enhances the safety of all facilitators, as they are likely to share information and intelligence to protect their interests.

Despite perceptions to the contrary, smuggling is not inherently violent. Due to smuggling's need to remain undetected, smuggling facilitators, like other individuals who perform criminalized activities, do their best to avoid the authorities' attention. Only one reference of competition-based antagonism among organizations was identified as part of data collection efforts in this sample. This case involved two groups providing border crossing services in the town of Nogales, on the Mexican side of the border. The incident involved a *bajón*—the "stealing" of a customer by another group. In this case two young men, who had initially agreed to use the services of the group coordinated by Javier *Guero* Tapia, were approached in the street by a recruiter from another group. The recruiter suggested Tapia's group was ineffective and invited the men to opt for his services instead. The men, who had grown weary of waiting for several days to cross the border with Tapia, went back to the safe house, thanked him for his services and moved into the other group's safe house.

Maria "N"—Tapia's assistant—had witnessed the encounter between the recruiter and the two men from afar. She called the mother of the other recruiter over the phone, warning her about the dangers and the consequences of stealing other groups' people. "You bunch of idiots won't even know what hit you, so just watch out!" While the record shows Tapia and Maria were upset over the loss, there was no evidence of retaliation on the part of either group (Marquez, G. 2008. Personal Interview, Phoenix, Arizona).

Despite incidents like this, acts of escalated violence among human smuggling facilitators appear to be relatively uncommon, mostly due to the cooperative, non-hierarchical nature of smuggling and the community-based nature of the activity, which depends on the maintenance of social ties. Good interactions among neighbors allow a smuggling participant to ask for permission to house immigrants in transit for a night in exchange for a couple of hundred dollars; a mechanic can conduct an after-hours, unexpected car repair and wait on payment for a few days. Conflict among members is also infrequent as facilitators pose no threat of competition due to the specialized nature of smuggling tasks.

Limited financial profits

The cases analyzed show that individuals involved in smuggling were not able to save money consistently, and that their profits never translated into economic upward mobility. Profits from an individual's participation in human smuggling tend to be almost immediately re-circulated into the local economy. The relatively small returns smuggling generates were destined to cover rent, car repairs, food, medical bills, previously acquired debt, etc. In one case, a US$200 payment was used to cover the graduation expenses of a child graduating from high school (Maricopa County v. Martinez Ponce 2007, motion, aggravated circumstances). Most smuggling activities surveyed in this sample generated returns in the range of US$50 to US$200 to those who performed them. Considering smuggling activities are not characterized by their continuity or stability, participants cannot count on this income as regular, and so they are forced to rely on additional forms of employment.

While returns may be low, participation in the transit of undocumented immigrants is seen within migrant communities as a benign, valuable service provided on *behalf of* the facilitator's own ethnic group, and those who deliver with efficacy and promptitude are most likely rewarded with continuous requests for additional transit services from grateful, discrete and—most importantly—paying customers. And while returns are not necessarily constant or easy to come by, facilitators gain social status within their communities through their actions and treatment of border crossers.

Leaving smuggling

Since the careers of smuggling facilitators in this sample were all brought to a halt—at least temporarily—as a result of their arrests, little is known about the specific stresses that would force a smuggling facilitator to quit the business, or about facilitators' transition from smuggling into other occupations.

Most facilitators are aware of the sporadic nature of smuggling. In the narratives, operations are never described as a permanent, single, long-term occupation, although this may be a reflection of the size of the sample. People thought of smuggling as a temporary side job, a task that was performed only until something better (a higher paying job, for example) came up. References to "careers" in smuggling (that is, spanning over months or even years) are almost non-existent in the sample; these are basically restricted to coordinators, who have managed to create a strong community presence and who hold, in addition to their participation, positions that facilitate their contact with would-be migrants and their relatives and families. Most facilitators had collaborated with their groups only occasionally (in fact, for the majority of the facilitators who worked at safe houses and for the drivers recruited among customers, the one experience leading to their arrest constituted the whole extent of their involvement in smuggling). Few facilitators reported having been involved in smuggling for a long period of time. (This was most likely because many were immigrants who had only recently entered the country and who, unlike coordinators, lacked well-developed social ties in their new home.)

The range of expertise in smuggling among the facilitators in this sample ranged from having no prior experience (as in the case of undocumented immigrants requested by smugglers to perform driving or housekeeping activities as a one-time occurrence), to occasional participation (as in the case of some repeat drivers), to constant involvement over a span of several years (particularly among the men and women who conducted financial operations and recruitment, or who held a coordination-like role within the group). Still, the size of the sample does not allow for conclusions about the length of an individual's career in smuggling.

The arrest and conviction of individuals detained in the context of smuggling operations should not be interpreted as a definite end of their participation in the business, as some facilitators reported that they continued participating in smuggling activities despite negative experiences (encounters with law enforcement, detention and even prior smuggling convictions, etc.) Additional research is needed to examine smugglers' experiences following their convictions and the impact of incarceration on smuggling recidivism. Due to their lack of employment eligibility, smuggling facilitators post-conviction most likely re-enter the underground economy performing low-paying jobs, or making use of the skills acquired in their participation in smuggling to integrate into a new group in a different location, although this conclusion is merely conjectural.[4]

Conclusions

The cases in this sample reveal that smuggling constitutes—more than an act of economic exploitation or a national security threat—a supplemental income-earning mechanism for the poor which has been criminalized by the state. The forms in which the men and women in this sample organize, support and even enter into conflict with one another suggest that, far from being a criminal enterprise, smuggling is an activity of a social nature like any other, shaped not only by the markets' unique risks and challenges but also by the personalities of its participants. Smuggling organizations are made up by loosely affiliated individuals whose collaborations are characterized by the provision of specialized tasks, for reasons other than financial gain. For many facilitators, their participation was their way of paying back the favors others had done for them during their own migratory journeys; for many others, it was a way to gain social status and recognition, which in their view was much more important than generating or accumulating wealth. The constant references to smuggling as a favor done on behalf of others is further evidence of the market's community-based nature and raises questions about the implication on the social fabric of the law enforcement activities carried out to dismantle operations.

Smuggling operations are skillfully used by the media and the government to represent and criminalize not only an activity, but the population that facilitates it. And so characterizations of smuggling as an exploitative or violent market frequently mobilize representations of men and women abusing others like themselves, holding them against their will at safe houses, perpetrating isolated incidents of violence and putting them at risk during high-speed chases. And yet, aside from these graphic images, we know little about the kinds of violence faced by irregular immigrants in their interactions with smuggling facilitators as clients. Contrary to the media representations, testimonies suggest the majority of migratory journeys are safe and uneventful, with customers experiencing little or no violence at all—although their travels take place under precarious and many times dangerous circumstances.

In Phoenix, smuggling has become a lifeline to local subsistence for a segment of the city's working class, migrant population. While participation in smuggling is, for most participants, profit-driven, it is consistently interconnected with wider notions of morality (Galemba 2012b, 719). While they recognize the illicit nature of their actions, facilitators do not consider their work to pose any ethical challenges or contradictions. Instead, they take pride in their involvement in smuggling as a way to help others, as a means to support their families and as the mechanism that allows for the extralegal crossings of irregular migrants, many of whom are their own family and friends. As Galemba (2012b, 719) identified during her fieldwork among corn smugglers, for its participants human smuggling constitutes a legitimate source of employment in the context of a country that is unlikely to modify its border control practices—that is, where the likelihood of legal paths to migration opening is slim—and where the economic options that might actually improve household economies are extremely limited.

The earnings connected to smuggling are not high, resulting in limited competition or violence among facilitators. Border enforcement and hyper-vigilance instead play a more central role in determining the logistical and economic decisions of smuggling facilitators, which may in turn carry implications for the security of their clients. While they vehemently deny reports that they frequently abandon clients in the desert or abuse them while in transit, facilitators seem to have little hesitation in entrusting entire groups of migrants to clients seeking a reduction in their fees. This practice, perhaps aimed at reducing risks (that is, the likelihood of detection and arrest for facilitators themselves), reveals important changes in the protection-based relationship that lay at the core of the provision of smuggling services. By assuming a facilitation role, clients face increased exposure to law enforcement, becoming more likely to encounter dramatic legal repercussions. It is therefore important to look beyond the stereotypical forms of victimization associated with smuggling (which, while graphic, do not reflect the dimension of the relationship between facilitators and their clients) and the academic narratives that suggest high levels of sophistication and structure in smuggling which over time have facilitated the criminalization of migration. In this sense, participation in smuggling docs not merely constitute a form of resistance of the kind scholars like Spener (2009a) have theorized, given its drastic implications. Instead, the "success" of smuggling has been the result of its effectiveness at generating sources of employment and income—even when unreliable, inconsistent or even delusive—for the working poor. What is truly at stake, however, are the mechanisms that once allowed migrants to travel reliably, and which are at risk of being dangerously transformed due to ongoing efforts by the state to hyper-police and criminalize mobility.

Notes

1 Women's experiences in human smuggling are explored in Chapter 5.
2 According to case files, sudden, unexpected requests for help from border crossers in transit are more likely to take place among smuggling groups facilitating the transit of groups of considerable size. The first case prosecuted under the Coyote Law, for example, involved a group of 53 men and women who were trying to reach Phoenix by car. The driver was offered a US$500 reduction on his fee for his assistance.
3 Following the US immigration reform of 1996, an irregular migrant arrested while re-entering the country without proper documentation can be charged with illegal re-entry. However, the practice only became systematically implemented during the Obama administration. Currently the majority of irregular migrants in federal detention in the US are awaiting illegal re-entry processes (Human Rights Watch 2013). By 2010, the exceedingly large number of cases pending for prosecution had caused a considerable caseload backup in immigration courts nationwide, and forced the Immigration and Customs Enforcement branch of the US Department of Homeland Security to review its illegal re-entry enforcement policies and procedures.
4 Roman Robaina, convicted of leading a smuggling group, was sentenced to prison but his sentence was suspended after one year. He was assumed to have re-established his contacts and to have moved his operations to Mexico, where he was unlikely to face prosecution.

5 Gendering smuggling

Women and the facilitation of extralegal border crossings

> She did not know for how long she lingered in confusion, yet she overcame her panic and intuited that it did not matter where she was going or how fast she was heading, that eventually she would get to wherever she had to arrive. She smiled. She felt herself smile.
>
> They arrived to the other side. They lied on the shore, panting. It had only been a few meters [. . .].
>
> Chucho stood up, turned to look at the city behind them and said, "Well, what follows is easier."
>
> (Yuri Herrera 2010, *Señales que precederán al fin del mundo* [*Signs that will precede the end of the world*])

As I wait for my haircut in the crowded waiting area of *Bellos and Bellas* on a Saturday morning, I overhear Cynthia's conversation on the phone. Ramiro, one of her friends, has been arrested for smuggling. His wife does not speak English, and so she has relied on Cynthia to help her secure legal counsel for her husband. Cynthia calls an attorney about the arrest and arranges for him to visit Ramiro while in custody. The attorney also agrees to wait for payment, as he has known (and come to trust) Cynthia for some time. Cynthia calls back the desperate wife. There are children crying in the background. The woman herself breaks down and cries. "Things will be alright," Cynthia says. She also promises to stop by at some point this weekend, "just to see how you are doing." Cynthia hangs up, shakes her head in disappointment for a few seconds and then yells at me: "Are you ready yet?"

Cynthia spends a significant portion of her day connecting people through her job at the salon—she meets with the family members of potential border crossers to provide referrals, identifies drivers, talks to guides along the border, asks her own clients if they would like to make some money working for a few days as cooks or cleaning a house. Most of the work she performs—despite the time it involves—goes unpaid. Why does she do it?

Cynthia's beauty salon, in contrast with many other businesses in the same block in this predominantly working-class, Latino neighborhood in Phoenix, has remained open for over a decade. Despite the recent US economic downturn, Cynthia managed to open a second branch in a nearby neighborhood not too long ago, and a third salon in Las Vegas—over 600 kilometers from Phoenix—is about to open.

> Sometimes we cannot keep up, and so I have to go help the girls up the street; but I like Phoenix best. This is where I started cutting hair, and my kids grew up here. Besides, this is where everybody knows me.

Cynthia has over the years found an effective way to maintain her main source of income by connecting it to the provision of smuggling referrals, and assisting facilitators and their clients and families when they need *other* forms of help—she has lived in Phoenix for long enough to know doctors, nurses, school teachers, priests and police officers; used car dealers, apartment complex managers; the locations of thrift stores and food banks; churches and car shops; the owners of small restaurants and cleaning services. She is right: *everybody* knows her.

I sit in her chair. Cynthia's hands already show the devastating signs of rheumatoid arthritis. At 50, she relies on medication in order to get through her workday. She has no medical insurance, but this morning on her way in she got a steroid injection at a local pharmacy and she is feeling well. She has a long day ahead, taking her usual clients and also doing hair and makeup for a bridal party. I hold her hands and ask her how she is doing overall. She smiles warmly at me, looks at her hands with sadness and says:

> I have been getting sick too often lately and I am starting to worry that soon I will no longer be able to work. But I am not *too* worried, you know . . . by now I know enough people in Phoenix. It is not like when we first got here and nobody knew us and we had to start this business from scratch. I have been in this for a long time. If the time comes when I am too sick to work, I am going to know who to call. People owe me favors. When people needed to cross, we were here to help them. Besides, you know? I have always worked. This [she shows me her red, peeling hands] is not going to stop me.

In Phoenix, smuggling has become a lifeline to the local subsistence of many of the city's Latino working-class families like Cynthia's, who as a single mother of three has worked alongside her sister not only in their chain of small, low-priced beauty salons, but also at assisting smuggling facilitators with their tasks. Cynthia is proud of the work she does, and has hardly ever demanded compensation for it.

> Yes, I get some business through it, but I do it because I like it, because it is good for people to know they have someone they can trust. I watch the news every night, right—do you? —and I see how people are treated at some drop houses, that they don't give them food, or they are not given water, things like those. But that is not how we do things, you see? [She points at the small one-story brick house across the street from the salon] Like that house right there, can you see it? Well, that is a drop house. And if you go in you will find out that people are just there, watching TV, waiting. I get them a lady who goes fix their meals. The house is clean. She keeps it clean. And we keep the houses in good shape. And if anything goes wrong you can just come and let me know . . . you just call me and let me know.

Her reputation precedes her—and she knows it. Known throughout the city for her ability to facilitate border crossings, Cynthia has been the recruiter behind the journeys of multiple families, adults and children in Phoenix, often taking calls from other states requesting services. She does not hesitate to reprimand a guard the same way she calls out a client who has failed to abide by the terms of the verbal agreement or a coordinator who has kept a group of border crossers for too long. She will invite a driver to her son's graduation party or pick up—and pay for—over-the-counter medication for a client who has just arrived in Phoenix. "As the saying goes, *God helps those who help themselves*, right? I do not think I do anything wrong. We just work hard. We are just helping people."

Frequently overlooked in the rhetoric of border protection, and often underestimated actors in human smuggling characterizations—where male facilitators are prominently portrayed as violent, sex-crazed and bloodthirsty smugglers preying upon the weak, vulnerable, virginal woman in transit—women play a central role as providers of extralegal border crossing services. Far from remaining on the margins, women recruit potential clients; negotiate fees and payment plans; and withdraw deposits from banks and wire transfer stores. Some work cleaning safe houses, while others are known to deliver food and water. There are also women who drive border crossers in their own vehicles, and even anecdotal accounts of those who guide groups of migrants through the desert to safety.

Despite the importance of women's participation in human smuggling, their roles have hardly been the subject of empirical work—let alone theorization. The few accounts of women's participation available—which invariably appear following a smuggling tragedy, or in the context of explorations of sex trafficking and/or prostitution—tend to describe women as highly opportunistic individuals who, not unlike male human smugglers, take advantage of the vulnerability of migrant crossers to exploit them, or of the naïveté of young and unexperienced girls to condemn them to the inferno of the sex trade. And so aside from the most sensationalistic and tragic accounts or stereotypical narratives of madams and brothels, the roles of women in human smuggling have remained fundamentally unexplored.

This chapter describes the tasks, motivations and challenges of women in the context of their participation in human smuggling operations. Data reveal the distinctive gendered nature of the smuggling market, where women's visibility is key to generating business and completing financial tasks. While women join the smuggling market in a fashion similar to that of men—that is, via acquaintances and through their personal efforts to conduct business—often their participation comes through the existence or the establishment of familial or romantic ties.

Gender has implications upon what can be characterized as one of the most pressing challenges women face in their participation in smuggling: violence at the hands of other facilitators (mostly those they live with, like male relatives and romantic partners). While the smuggling market cannot be characterized as inherently violent, many women participating in smuggling become the target of aggression (verbal and physical) emerging from their personal relationships with other facilitators, rather than from their business interactions with clients. Most women are also mothers, primarily of US-born children, and are in the country extralegally. The irregular nature of their immigration status poses significant challenges to their families' lives in the event of an arrest—family separation, deportation, incarceration—at a level not faced by male facilitators, who are more likely to be single or to support families abroad, rather than locally. The intensity of the local law enforcement immigration control efforts has also targeted women disproportionately, surveillance and intimidation often extended to their children, regardless of their immigration status. The chapter explores these aspects and experiences, relying on narratives present in court documents and on the testimonies of women in an attempt to explore the interplay of gender and the facilitation of irregular border crossings.

Women in smuggling

Out of the 66 facilitators surveyed as part of this project, only 12 were women. Their ages spanned from 18 to 62, while the majority of men were concentrated in the 28 to 33 year-old group. These age spans suggest women are more likely to join smuggling operations at a younger age and to remain involved for longer periods of time, while men's involvement may be limited to periods of time when significant amounts of physical energy are needed (trekking through the desert, guiding groups, driving cross-country, security, etc.).[1] Women's activities had a tendency to be performed primarily indoors and locally. Women also tended to be more educated than men, who on average had a ninth-grade education. Two women in this sample had completed trade school, and one had enrolled in university for a semester. Women were also more likely to have a higher level of English proficiency than men.

Most women had long-standing stories of residence in the US, having migrated (largely extralegally) many years prior to the start of their involvement in smuggling. This fact proved to be particularly significant as men often had much shorter histories of in-country residence, having lived in the US temporarily or seasonally (only a handful of men had lived in the US for more than a few months by the time of their smuggling-related arrest).[2] While every single woman in this study lived and worked in the immediacy of her neighborhood—and was highly aware of the resources available to her disposal and that of her family—most men had traveled from out of the state of Arizona in order to facilitate transportation services, and had limited local awareness of the social and community landscape.

In terms of employment, women also had a higher tendency to have a more stable, long-term job history than men. Women were more likely to work for established businesses in the regular economy (rather than being self-employed or depending on day-to-day labor, as many men did), mostly in the service industry. By virtue of being employees of large companies, many women had access to bank accounts, which allowed them to get paid—but which they also used to receive smuggling fee deposits. Women seemed to have far greater financial knowledge than men. The majority of those involved in the financial aspects of smuggling were women.

Another important aspect of women's experience in smuggling was parenthood—most specifically in the context of their status as irregular migrants and single heads of mixed-status households. (Of the 12 women in the study, 11 were indeed undocumented.) The majority of the women had children, most of whom were US-born. Significant resources and energies were devoted to children's wellbeing and education, primarily because of the ever-present threat of deportation that could follow a random police encounter.

While most women resided with and cared for their children in Arizona, most men with children lived on their own, childcare not being much of a concern. Furthermore, the children and spouses of the majority of men resided primarily out of the country. In the event of an arrest and the ensuing deportation, while most men could reunite with their families in their country of origin, most women were often irreparably separated from their children. Taking these aspects into consideration, women's position in smuggling was significantly more precarious than that of men.

Women's tasks in smuggling

In the same way popular images of irregular migrants along the US–Mexico border tend to be masculinized, human smuggling tends to be primarily constructed as a male-dominated occupation, under the control of hyper-violent, hyper-sexual men who abuse those who travel under their watch, driving them along inhospitable regions in dangerous and negligent ways, and exploiting them financially after inflicting physical, emotional or sexual torture upon them.

These perceptions have permeated law enforcement approaches to enforcing human smuggling laws, while further allowing for women's experiences (as both border crossers and facilitators of such crossings) to be rendered invisible. Most of those participating in smuggling and arrested as a result of enforcement actions are men. Women, on the other hand, are arrested with less frequency, yet their absence in numbers should not be interpreted as an indicator of non or peripheral involvement. Women perform essential tasks in the completion of successful border crossings, like recruiting potential clients, conducting verbal agreement negotiations, providing room and board for migrants in transit and assisting them with their day-to-day needs by cleaning the safe houses where they stay and fixing their meals. Women are indeed highly active in the provision of crossings, responsible for a significant amount of the interactions between facilitators and border crossers.

In prior chapters, smuggling has been defined as reliant on highly individualized tasking. I will further argue that tasking in smuggling is also highly gendered. Tasks like cooking, cleaning, check cashing and arranging for/hosting migrants in transit tend to be largely feminized (often dismissed by male facilitators as mere "assistance" and not constituting full-fledged tasks, despite the fact that they are central to the success of any border crossing journey) and are therefore mostly assigned to women for minimal compensation, or to male migrants working at safe houses trying to pay off their fees. The more visible and higher paid tasks of driving, trekking and providing security, which are also the ones most often associated with human smuggling, are primarily performed by men. Perhaps the main way in which the gendered hierarchy of smuggling is operationalized is through salaries: women's compensation in smuggling is significantly less than that of men. Women must often work more hours in order to generate the same earnings as men, even when the task performed is similar.

Perceptions connected with gender—those labeling women as more social, caring, protective, etc.—also play a role in the distribution of tasks in smuggling (Hagan 2008). It is assumed that women are inherently nurturing, willing to protect those who may be vulnerable or in situations of perceived need (Zhang 2007; Zhang et al. 2007)—a protection that will be extended to those crossing the border under their watch. This notion is often mobilized by facilitators—both male and female alike—to create business opportunities by portraying the services coordinated by women as safer, more reliable. Women have in fact created a niche in smuggling by mobilizing and effectively selling perceptions of protection, care and reliability (see Hagan 2008; Zhang et al. 2007).

Creating the perception of protection and care is a time-consuming activity, yet one that can have the potential of generating further business—and, therefore, income. One of the acts for which women are most often remembered by those who cross borders irregularly is in fact their level of caregiving and attention.

At 62, Mrs Dolores Quintas was the eldest woman among those working in the facilitation of border crossings in Arizona. Born in Mexico, Mrs Quintas had collaborated for several years with a group of guides by housing one or two migrants in transit at a time in her small apartment in Phoenix. Following her arrest, a border crosser she housed commented on his experience:

> She was a very nice lady; the coyotes took us to her place after they found out the police had identified the safe house. The coyotes walked right into her apartment saying they would have to spend the night there, along with my friend and I. And so Mrs Quintas got angry because the coyotes walked into her place with their guns. She told them, "You are only scaring these kids. They can stay but not you. Take your guns with you. And I will never, never allow for that kind of disrespect in my home, no matter how much you pay." Once the coyotes were gone, Mrs Quintas fed my friend and I, and then set up blankets in the kitchen so that we could spend the night. She fed us breakfast the next day along with two other women who were also very nice to us and before someone else stopped to pick us up. We never saw her again.
>
> (Maricopa County v. Becerra-Robles, 2009, p. 3–4)

In legal documents, the two border crossers housed by Quintas—who were eventually charged with committing their own human smuggling—not only spoke of her in terms of her role of providing them with housing, but they also emphasized the sense of protection and safety they felt while in her home, and her efforts to protect them from the terrified guards. While both men were charged, they refused to identify Mrs Quintas as a smuggler: "She took us in, gave us blankets and fed us. We were never in danger."

While the two men staying at Mrs Quintas' residence described her actions as protective, there are other mechanisms in place to more formally increase the levels of protection of border crossers and their families. There is a particular category of services referred to in the data as *primera* (first). This service, which in this sample was provided largely by women, further indicates the existence of specific degrees of specialization in smuggling. It involves the sale, at a much higher rate, of faster, more efficient border crossing transits services to those who travel extralegally.

Typically these specialized services are facilitated on behalf of infants and children, pregnant women and elderly or sick migrants, and imply expedited border crossing services through the use of shorter, more direct routes. They are also marketed—and sold—as relying on methods or using mechanisms to reduce, or even altogether eliminate, the likelihood of detection by law enforcement (crossing a checkpoint using authentic documentation; being crossed with the assistance of, or by, a complicit border official; flying in small planes; traveling in official vehicles not subjected to inspection, etc.). But most significantly, and especially in the case of Arizona, a specialized crossing translates into a dramatic reduction in the amount of travel time, limiting the exposure of border crossers to the desert elements. These services, by virtue of reducing crossing times, are marketed as extremely safe and offering high levels of care and protection, so it is not surprising that they are also often marketed, coordinated and provided by women, who are regarded as naturally inclined to provide care and protection to the vulnerable.

Facilitators providing *primera* services only take referrals from past clients or other facilitators. Payment—contrary to more regular transits, for which installments and terms can be negotiated—is most often due in advance; the services are also guaranteed. The following conversation between two coordinators—one in charge of arranging crossings through the desert and a woman who worked exclusively transporting pregnant women—reveals some of the dynamics of these services:

Facilitator 1 (F1): Thank you for taking my call, I imagine you must be busy.
Facilitator 2 (F2): Don't mention it. So you said you have a young lady for me?
F1: I do! You know my rules: no children and no pregnant women to the other side [through the desert]. I am not going to put a mother or her baby in danger.
F2: No, no. I understand, my friend. It is very dangerous to bring across a woman in such delicate condition. How far [into her pregnancy] is she?
F1: Seven months. Her feet swell up, and she can't walk much.
F2: Poor thing! You don't want her to suffer, no way.
F1: So, what do you recommend?
F2: Check with the husband first, to see if he is OK with it. It is more expensive, yes. But she will only have to walk from the house on this side of the border to the other. The two houses are connected by a tunnel. She comes in through one side, comes out the other, gets in the van and that's all! Three hours later she is in Phoenix. No walks, no danger, no *migra*[3], nothing!

F1:   But how will he know she is OK?

F2:   You know all trips are guaranteed. We have good vehicles, all of them air-conditioned. We have someone check the women here at the house before they leave, to make sure they are OK. Most importantly, she will be in [Phoenix] before her husband! [*Laughs*]

F1:   Thank you, he is very worried about her.

F2:   Please tell him his wife will be taken care of, that she will be safe. You should tell him this is all we do, that *we only transport pregnant women*, and that people trust us because we take good care of them.

The cost of transporting a pregnant woman was, at the time this conversation took place, about three times that of a standard crossing (while the woman's husband paid US$1600 for his journey from Nogales, Sonora, to Phoenix, Arizona, his wife's fee amounted to US$4200—a price families justify and are eager to pay in their efforts to protect their loved ones).[4]

Not only do women arrange for the provision of *primera* services by coordinating their logistics, they are also overrepresented among those convicted for financial crimes performed in connection with human smuggling—charges ranging from the ever-present "money laundering" to the cryptic "use of electronic equipment in the commission of a crime of human smuggling" (in other words, a cell phone). These processes, while often described in law enforcement reports as complex and structured operations, are instead characterized by their high frequency and relative ease. They involve the online- or cell phone-based verification that a deposit involving smuggling fees has been made to a specific account. Once the deposit has been verified, it is ready to be withdrawn.

The reason financial tasks were most often entrusted to women appeared to be because of the higher ownership among women of bank accounts compared to that of men. Women were more likely to have official forms of identification than men (as they were often employed by corporations or firms that issue identity or employee identification cards; they also reported having voting registration or consular cards from their countries of origin, which are recognized by some US banks as a valid form of identification). These identifications can be used to open legitimate bank accounts. All women convicted of financial crimes did use the accounts for their personal finances, but would occasionally "lend" their accounts for the reception of smuggling fees.

While many men also had access to identification cards and bank accounts, it seems that women had what prosecutors considered a logistical advantage: they were often more financially savvy than men; the number and size of banking transactions many women handled have been used as an indicator of their degree of financial sophistication. There was no indication, however, of women conducting any other type of financial transaction aside from deposits or transfers. Furthermore, none of them reaped significant financial returns for their efforts—each bank or money wire business visit typically earned women an average of US$50.

Martha Rosas, a 22 year old, narrated her experience of withdrawing deposits, and the use she made of her earnings:

> *Crazy* calls once a client tells him the money is in; I check my account and verify [that] the deposit has in fact been made. If it is in, *Crazy* asks me to meet him at the bank and I withdraw the money and I give it to him. He pays me $50 per every [sic] withdrawal I help him with. In a month I can make about $200, $250. The best month I had I made $500. It depends how many people they cross. I used the money to make my car payment—I have a small Ford. I also use the money to pay for gas and for my other monthly bills.

The motives behind smuggling

As described in Chapter 3, the reasons cited among facilitators for their involvement in smuggling are many and varied—from generating supplementary income to repaying or paying forward past favors, supporting family members' efforts or helping people in need.

And yet, among female facilitators, altruistic notions did not figure high in their list of motivators. Women consistently explained their participation in smuggling as driven purely by financial need—as a way to benefit financially—through the generation of additional income, even if only supplemental. Most women clearly articulated the monetary or in-kind value of their contributions and, unlike some male facilitators, did not appear to define their work as favors performed on behalf of others. Women, as well as men, spoke of their participation as constituting a legitimate form of labor performed on behalf of clients, one that ought to be compensated.

Aware that, given its gendered nature, their potential to generate earnings in human smuggling is connected to the kinds of roles they perform, some women often opted to be paid less—or not at all—for their collaborations. Successful border crossings could eventually translate into significant social capital and increased status that could be cashed in at times of need. For several women, this was an issue of investing, as well as one of customer relations. Rosa explained:

> There was a time when I did not have money to pay for rent. I called German and I told him about it, and he just said he would give me the money I needed to pay for that month. I know I am in a position to do this because plenty of times I have gotten people for them and they do not always pay me, but then I know that when I need help, German and his brother will be there for me.

Aside from monetary profits and the possibility of acquiring significant levels of clout in their communities, women also conceptualized their participation as motivated by gendered expectations and cultural obligations. The care of ailing parents or children, or supporting or assisting other relatives or friends through the facilitation of crossings frequently required a level of flexibility and amount of time that jobs in the formal economy did not always allow for. That was why smuggling came in handy. The nature of smuggling tasks allowed many women to work from their homes, so they were able to spend more time with their children and other relatives, providing additional childcare support, or assisting with household chores and smuggling tasks.

For Joanna Lopez, for example, smuggling afforded her the ability to care for her chronically ill child. Unable to support her two daughters on her salary as a janitor, Joanna took a second job which required her to spend daytime hours away from her daughter. The child was cared for by her grandfather—the author of a letter to the judge asking for a reduced sentence for his daughter:

> Dear Sir
>
> [My daughter] Joanna Lopez is hard working—she worked as a janitor, besides she is a good mother of two daughters, one is sick with an ulcer, she does not live with the husband, she has suffered of [sic] domestic violence, that is why I beg for your understanding to grant her freedom.
>
> (Maricopa County v. Lopez-Guiron, 2006)

The income Lopez generated via her participation in smuggling (US$50 per night per person in transit) was the equivalent to an entire day of work away from her daughters. Smuggling allowed her not only to spend a considerable amount of time at home but also to care for her own daughters on a more regular basis while saving money. Joanna estimated her smuggling-related earnings to be in the range of US$200 per month—an amount not much different from the salary she would earn over an entire week as a janitor.

Participation in smuggling also allowed female facilitators to promote, maintain or expand their day jobs or businesses in the formal economy. As described in this chapter's introduction, Cynthia and her sister were able to keep their beauty salon open at the peak of the US economic downturn—in fact, they even managed to open two other branches (one in Phoenix and a second in Nevada)—where they would offer, alongside perms and haircuts, smuggling referral services.

Renata Jimenez navigated through a period of limited work hours at the catering company where she worked by allowing a friend to use her bank account for the deposit of smuggling fees. Renata received deposits from multiple US states, ranging from a few hundred to a couple of thousand dollars. She was paid US$50 for every withdrawal she conducted.

Her work hours at the company eventually increased, although she continued assisting her friend with occasional deposits, earning a couple of hundred dollars per month, according to her statements as well as legal case documents. Renata's actions allowed her to ride the wave of limited employment hours. She was eventually able to purchase a low-cost franchise to start her own janitorial business, which she had just launched at the time of her arrest (Maricopa County v. Saavedra-Trujillo, 2009).

Entry into smuggling

As in the case of men, most women enter smuggling through relatives, friends and acquaintances. These opportunities to participate are also of occasional, coincidental nature. Parents or siblings who have been involved in smuggling request assistance; coworkers or friends ask to process a withdrawal or for an extra pair of hands to clean a home; a neighbor offers compensation in exchange for borrowing a birth certificate or a driver's license which can facilitate a child or perhaps another woman's border crossing, etc. As in the case of men, opportunities are random, hardly ever continuous or systematic and do not constitute a significant source of income, being instead used as a form to supplement wages from other jobs or self-employment.

Women were also more likely than men to enter smuggling as part of their own entrepreneurial efforts—seeking opportunities for business that could be translated into monetary or in-kind earnings. Several women in fact had small businesses that they ran on their own, or had special skills or training that they mobilized to generate earnings.

Some women reportedly introduced their male partners into smuggling through their own personal connections or family businesses, as Susana Marquez explained:

> He didn't know anything when he came to me. He had been working as a cook at a restaurant but wanted to do something else. I was the one who taught him; I had been doing this for a long time with my brothers, and so he asked that I showed him how it was done—he had just moved to Arizona. So I sent him with my friend's husband, and they went to the border and he got to meet everybody who was doing something—the drivers, the walkers, the bill collectors, the recruiters. He just went around and asked questions, a lot of questions. A few years later we started fighting a lot because he was [seeing] other women and so I left him, and so now he is not that nice to me anymore, so I do not always like working with him.

The emergence or presence of romantic or spousal-like relationships as a path into smuggling, however, seemed to be more prevalent in the experiences of women than those of men. Many women reportedly assisted their romantic partners in the performance of smuggling services by executing tasks like cashing checks, delivering food or water to drop houses, verifying payment information, even guiding small groups at times. Others reported working alongside husbands or former spouses, in what were characterized as more central activities (recruiting customers and guides, for example), not establishing their roles along gender lines—instead, positioning themselves as equals, despite facing or having faced acts of violence:

> I divorced him a long time ago because he used to beat me and so I decided I didn't want to be with him anymore. But we had been in [smuggling] for a long time, even before the [newcomers] arrived. I always worked and I had my own money, but he was doing this on the side, so when somebody needed a favor, like picking up money or driving a group of people I would call him and tell him and he'd do it. I only did it because of [my] kids, they are his so he had to [find ways to help] support them. Now he is no longer in the business; he is lucky, he got out a couple of weeks before everybody we knew got arrested, but it was because he was very sick and weak and couldn't work anymore.

The gendered challenges of smuggling: violence, surveillance, parenting

Romantic involvement among providers in criminalized activities or underground markets has traditionally been characterized as exploitative of women, when not dismissed by scholars as a peripheral or even shallow incident. Women tend to be described in the literature of underground economies in quasi-pathological terms: as being in search of males who can provide protection; as escaping life-long sexual abuse or dysfunctional homes; or seeking to support a drug habit.[5] Yet none of the women in this sample fitted that profile. Most were in fact not involved in romantic relationships, supporting their children independently; while some worked limited hours, all 12 of the identified women were employed or self-employed. Not a single one reported drug or alcohol use or experimentation, and none had criminal backgrounds. If anything, their lives had in fact been more stable than those of many male facilitators, who had to move constantly and depend on seasonal or sporadic job offers. The cases did reflect, however, that in smuggling men as well as women do engage in relationships (romantic or not) characterized by tremendous power differentials, where women often tend to be in more vulnerable situations than men, as these are more likely to be involved in the facilitation of women's extralegal border crossings. The most serious cases of violence involving women facilitators as perpetrators had a tendency to occur in the context of kidnapping cases.

While women hardly ever figured among those working at safe houses where kidnappings and other acts of violence took place,[6] the case of Ana Ramos is relevant given the extent of her involvement and the severity of the acts in question. She was identified as a member of a group that offered services to unsuspecting crossers in small towns along the border in Mexico with the promise of transporting them to Phoenix. Once in town, the migrants were stripped of shoes and clothing and locked in a room pending the payment of fees, higher than those initially agreed upon. When migrants were unable to pay, they were not only threatened, but also often physically hurt. Ramos' role was to make ransom calls to the families of the migrants being held.

A single mother of four, Ana had left her children in the care of her mother in a small town in Northern Mexico. She arrived at the US–Mexico border without any kind of monetary backing or references to finance her extralegal journey into the US. Her goal was to cross the border in order to obtain employment that would enable her to support her children, despite the fact that she had extremely limited experience in the workforce. Her only job experience amounted to her days as a helper at a market stall. With a fifth-grade education, her inability to read or write and her extreme shyness, her employment options were limited.

Once at the border, Ana identified a smuggling group that offered to transport her to Phoenix. Under the terms of her smuggling agreement, she was to perform cleaning and cooking duties in exchange for transportation into the city, although she was never informed of how long she would have to work in order to fulfill the agreement. From the legal case file, it is inferred that during her time at the safe house Ana became romantically involved with a man who often gave instructions to the guards.

It is not clear on the basis of the legal documents alone whether Ana's permanence at the safe house was out of obligation or by choice. Some documents suggest that she was not allowed to leave the premises—unlike men who reportedly worked off their fees and were then allowed to continue with their journeys. One of the legal documents indicates that Ana was instead forced to stay and was only allowed to leave the safe house in the company of other males in order to buy groceries for the safe house occupants (Maricopa County v. Arriaga-Ortiz, 2009, Presentence report p. 1).

During her time at the safe house, Ana also became pregnant. As her pregnancy progressed, Ana began to notice signs of fetal distress. However, her romantic partner—to whom she referred as her husband—did not allow her to leave the safe house to seek medical care, nor did he offer to take her to the local hospital. Ana eventually miscarried.

Ana's voice in the legal process was largely silenced by the nature of the offense that took place at the safe house where she stayed and by the court's narrative, which established her as one of the brains of a "highly complex kidnapping operation." Yet during the investigation that followed her arrest, Ana repeatedly attributed her fear of the city as the reason for her staying with the group. While she stated that she was not held against her will, she repeatedly claimed that she "didn't know anybody who could help" and "was scared of wandering into a city I did not know" (Maricopa County v. Arriaga-Ortiz, 2009, Presentence report, p. 2).

Ana's case is relevant to women's experiences of border crossings because of the implications of her relationship with those in charge of her transit. While multiple women in this study also disclosed that they had experienced significant domestic violence events involving their romantic partners, none of them had initiated their relationships in the context of their border crossing journeys, as Ana had. Most women referred to their experiences of domestic abuse as eventually leading to their independence, economic growth and overall empowerment. In contrast, Ana endured a level of violence and victimization that was consistently ignored during the legal process and was never raised by her defense or the court officer responsible for writing her sentencing recommendation.

Ana's experience was used instead throughout the legal process as evidence to support her vilification. She was described as a violent, profit-driven individual who was in charge of making calls to the families of those being held at the safe house, threatening them with inflicting serious bodily harm to the victim in the event that the smuggling fees were not immediately paid. Ana's involvement with the coordinator (a college-educated man from Mexico) was also consistently characterized as evidence of her criminal intentions. But it was her status as an irregular migrant that earned her a prison recommendation, when her status was constructed as a contributing factor to her criminal activity and her likelihood to reoffend. Her sentencing recommendation suggested her criminogenic risk factors were mainly associated to her undocumented status. At 21, Ana Ramos was convicted for her involvement in the kidnapping of a Mexican man, and sentenced to one year in prison (Maricopa County v. Arriaga-Ortiz, 2009. *Plea Agreement*).

The processes by which women's actions are criminalized by the state are not uniquely related to the construction of their participation in violent crimes.

Hyper-surveillance and patrolling in predominantly migrant neighborhoods have also played a role in the efforts to intimidate women and children. While MCSO is known to operate along the periphery of Maricopa County, the Phoenix Police Department conducts the majority of its activities within urban settings. On October 26, 2009, Isabel Medina-Meraz, a single mother of two US-born children who ran a small house-cleaning operation in the Phoenix area, was on her way to work when two Phoenix police officers began to follow her vehicle. The officers referred to Medina's behavior as suspicious: "The driver look[ed] in our direction. When she did this she seemed startled and then immediately looked away and stared straight ahead with her hands locked rigidly on the steering wheel" (Maricopa County v. Medina Meraz 2009, Police Report p. 1). The officers did not proceed to make a stop at that point. Instead, Officer Schiaveto continued to follow her from a close distance:

> I made a U-turn and attempted to catch up with the vehicle to run a registration check; *the plates were valid.* As soon as we made our U-turn we tried to get behind the vehicle. As we made the turn the vehicle had pulled in front of a house.

Despite having verified the validity of the plates, the two officers continued to follow Medina-Meraz, without having established probable cause, and waited outside of her home and as she drove through her neighborhood:

> We waited until the vehicle left the house and later the vehicle drove by. When it made the turn it failed to use a turn signal. We directed our patrol car behind the vehicle and again the vehicle made an abrupt turn into a parking lot failing to use its turn signal.

It was only at this time (according to the police report, 45 minutes from the time of initial contact) that the officers decided to make a stop. The officer had up to this point not identified a reason for his suspicion, nor determined probable cause. It was only when a minimal traffic violation was committed that the officer decided to approach the vehicle—which had already parked—its occupants (Medina-Meraz and her companion), already walking into two different stores. It was this behavior that the officers characterized as "suspicious" and used to justify the stop.

   The officers proceeded to question Medina-Meraz and her companion, who "appeared nervous and were fidgety and looking all around." Feeling intimidated and fearing further questioning, Medina-Meraz incriminated herself and stated that until recently she had been involved in human smuggling by withdrawing money from bank accounts and receiving US$50 per transaction. The man driving the vehicle was an unemployed construction worker she had hired to help her with her house cleaning business and he had been working with her only for a couple of weeks. Meraz was handcuffed and taken away by police, who also arrested her companion—he was ultimately deported.

Medina-Meraz was not the only member of her family affected by her arrest. Following her detention, police placed her two minor children and their caregiver—a neighbor Medina-Meraz had listed as her emergency contact—under around-the-clock surveillance for unexplained reasons. Medina-Meraz's daughter, a 14-year-old minor, was followed to and from school, and one afternoon after school was stopped and questioned without parental consent by the same officers who had arrested her mother. The officers searched Medina-Meraz's daughter's backpack and confiscated one of her school notebooks, claiming the math calculations that appeared on several pages were most likely evidence of the child's mother's involvement in human smuggling. The minor stated she used the notebook to teach her younger sister how to count.

Police did not believe the child's account and instead argued that her mother was perhaps tied not only to a human but even to a drug smuggling organization. The allegations were used not only to justify the search, but also to intimidate the child, and to lead her into believing the questioning was perfectly normal given her mother's involvement in smuggling.

The children of women involved in smuggling often tend to be the targets of hyper-vigilance and intimidation. In two other separate cases encountered in this research, two women reported that their five children, all minors, were followed by law enforcement officers assigned to their mothers' cases on their way to and from school, while visiting friends, at social gatherings and to their own homes. As in Medina-Meraz's case, the children were also subjected to questioning and intimidation, and told that their lack of cooperation with the authorities could result in the incarceration of their mothers. In all cases, the children were questioned without the presence of a consenting adult or parent. One afternoon, Zenaida Armenta's two sons were held in their own home by law enforcement officers at a time when Armenta was still under investigation for her participation in smuggling but had not been charged. The children, who had consented to the officers entering their home, were not allowed to leave the room where they were being questioned until their mother returned home.

While most men in the sample worked to support families in Mexico (thirty men v. only two of the women), nine of the women reported having US-born children, compared to only six of the men. With the exception of a woman who was a naturalized US citizen, the rest were undocumented migrants. These numbers place the majority of women in this sample as members of mixed-status families (families consisting of individuals both with and without legal residence rights), a factor that impacted them in a much different way than men in terms of their ability to care for and support their families.

All respondents faced deportation to their country of origin following their release from detention. Yet while the families of most male respondents lived permanently in Mexico (allowing men the opportunity to reunite with them), for the majority of women their release signified the end of their ability to reside with their children, who were more likely to live in the United States and/or hold US citizenship. For many of these mixed-status families, the arrest of the mother implied not only a temporary separation, but most likely their inability to reunite under legal terms. As most women were undocumented, a smuggling conviction effectively eliminated their eligibility to regularize their immigration status in the future. This also translated into women losing any kind of eligibility for a border crossing permit that would allow them to at least visit their children. And having lost one, if not their main, household provider via a mother's arrest, the costs associated with a family's relocation following a release are prohibitive. Some women were however determined to re-enter the US illegally, despite the likelihood of re-arrest and harsh sentences, as they were convinced the economic and educational opportunities for their children were greater in the US:

> I have two boys; one is almost done with high school, the other one is still a baby. Both were born here. The oldest wants to be a doctor, but he had to get out of school when I got arrested so that he could support his baby brother. I know I am not supposed to come back after they kick me out, but I am going to cross back in anyways, I have made up my mind. I know I will not have a life, that my life will be that of a caged animal, not able to go anywhere, but I would much rather live that way than being away from my kids. I will come back to be with my children again.

Mothers who are arrested and convicted as a result of their participation in smuggling are, given their status as undocumented migrants, often deported without consideration for their children. Most women later return to their children with the assistance of smugglers themselves. Yet the likelihood of them being re-arrested is high, given the patrolling and surveillance to which the neighborhoods where they reside are subjected. And, as previously mentioned, illegal re-entry following a deportation is considered a criminal offense, punishable by imprisonment, which increases the pressure on women to maintain a clandestine, anomic life.

Conclusions

The series of interviews and data collected among male and female human smugglers in the Maricopa County area reveal that smuggling is mostly a horizontal, non-hierarchical, referral-based activity, typically conducted by its participants along with friends and family. Participation in smuggling, particularly among women, constitutes a supplemental income-generating activity, as it is carried out in addition to permanent and/or stable jobs in the free market. Smuggling's specialized tasking often allows women to participate around childcare or employment obligations without compromising their main source of income. Tasking is highly gendered, with the activities most commonly identified with smuggling— desert treks, driving, security enforcement, etc.—being performed by men. While women's roles in smuggling tend not to be as visible, they are also central to the success of every migrant's journey, as they involve recruitment, coordination, the provision of room and board and the execution of financial transactions. Compensation for services varied greatly between genders. Roles performed by men (drivers, guides, security) were paid at a much higher rate than the tasks performed by women, whose compensations were typically half of those received by men (an average of US$50 per person and/or transaction). Women working alongside their spouses or romantic partners were even less likely than single women or female heads of household to receive any kind of financial compensation for their collaboration.

The increase in female migration and "women led strategies for migration" (Landolt and Da 2005, 646; Spitzer et al. 2003; Teo 2003; Zhang et al. 2007, 704) would suggest there has been a renegotiation of familial and gender roles within migrant households as women are faced with competing values and demands (Spitzer et al. 2003, 267). In addition to the cultural and religious values that are frequently cited as elements shaping migrant women's gender roles as well as their moral and ethical selves (Spitzer et al. 2003, 269), involvement in a market labeled as illicit would become an added dimension of their socially constructed responsibilities. Yet human smuggling is an activity that does not carry the social stigma attached to other markets like prostitution or drug sales. Instead, it is perceived, particularly among immigrants, as a benevolent action carried out on behalf of the larger community. In this context, women's involvement in smuggling and the services they provide by caring for other women's needs, or assisting families in their reunification, are in line with the social expectations dictated upon their gender.

It is perhaps human smuggling's unique logistics that have facilitated the provision of specific roles by women. As a market depending on highly specialized tasks, work is not available on a continuous and/or permanent basis, but instead on the demand of a specific service by a collaborating smuggling operator. By providing a task perceived as feminine (protection) in a male-dominated market, women have been able to create their own business opportunities. Yet these tasks continue to rely on culturally held perceptions of females as providers of care and protection. Furthermore, it is important to note that participation in smuggling is not a catalyst for economic or social advancement among immigrant women. While a welcome source of income, smuggling continues to reinscribe women's roles as caregivers, and limits the roles available to them. The obligation of succeeding at smuggling has also become another responsibility imposed onto women.

The experiences of many of the women in smuggling are also defined by their gendered implications—many of which are not limited to the domestic space. Their incomes are significantly lower than those of men. Most women report having endured high levels of abuse in the context of their romantic relationships, which typically involve a smuggling provider. Arrests and convictions also impact women differently. A smuggling-related conviction typically leads to the deportation of the offender. While men are more likely to support families in their countries of origin, most women do so locally. Most men are eventually able to reunite with their families in their countries of origin following their release, while most women face the dilemma of separation. Unable to regularize their immigration status following a conviction for a felony offense, most women must decide between being away from their families and re-entering the country illegally, despite the drastic repercussions a re-arrest entails.

This study, as a qualitative inquiry into smuggling, has limitations. It only involves a very small sample of the universe of women involved in smuggling, and therefore should not be interpreted as representative of the experiences of all female smugglers. It is also limited geographically: the data are limited to the work of women in one of the many smuggling markets in the US. Work in other smuggling markets may reflect other gender-based trends not uncovered in this sample. This chapter does not include the perspectives of undocumented immigrants on their smuggling experiences, although their accounts informed some aspects of the smuggling process. While cognizant of the perils and challenges human smuggling involves for all parties, the consistent reliance on the services of smugglers on the part of undocumented immigrants serves as a clear indicator of its success, and of its permanence and relevance as part of the journeys of the poor, still unable to access the protections granted by visas and passports.

Notes

1 These tasks are not uniquely performed by men, as explained below. However, they are more likely to perform them in the context of smuggling.
2 This occurred in all cases, with the exception of those involving men who had been deported as a result of local immigration enforcement measures. They tended to have resided in the country for years or decades and to have established families.
3 A colloquial reference to the US Immigration Service or any of its agents assigned to the border.
4 Hagan (2008) has also documented the provision of specialized services for women and the efforts of male migrants to identify reliable smuggling facilitators who can provide special care to women in transit.
5 In his renowned ethnography of street drug dealers, Philip Bourgois describes romantic relationships among street drug dealers, portraying women as vulnerable and prone to engage in dysfunctional relationships responding to cultural tradition:

> At age thirteen, fleeing an abusive father, Candy was faithfully following [her] traditional cultural scenario [. . .] Instead of being protected from her abusive father and guided into a new male dominated household, Candy faced the closed corporate inner-city street gang, and she was raped by the adolescent boys that Felix, her future husband, led. [. . .] *Romantic love in a conjugal relationship enables a subordinated woman to assert her individual needs while at the same time binding her to the principle of a male-dominated nuclear household.*
>
> (Bourgois 2003, 219–223; my emphasis in italics)

6 Zhang et al. (2007, 701) argue, in their study of women's participation in transnational human smuggling, that "the limited place of violence and turf as organizing features of human smuggling" may actually contribute to the participation of women in smuggling, as this is not socially perceived as violating notions of what constitutes "appropriate" female behavior.

6 Conceptualizing violence in smuggling

Over the last decade, increasing reports of migrants' victimization along the Arizona/Sonora border have dominated the headlines. Journalistic and anecdotal accounts strongly suggest smuggling facilitators are behind these events, but no empirical research has been conducted to date to verify the extent of that assertion. Neither has research been conducted on the nature or prevalence of violence in human smuggling operations.

This chapter takes a structural approach to explaining violence in smuggling. Instead of focusing on a single actor—or perpetrator—it looks at violence as an element of the continuum of surveillance that surrounds human mobility along borders. I argue that smuggling violence constitutes only one of the multiple forms of violence that border crossers may face, and which, in addition to smuggling facilitators, has also been executed by the state. This is done primarily through immigration enforcement and the implementation of surveillance mechanisms and criminalizing laws. While in the case of Arizona the introduction of a law defining smuggling as a crime sought to stop the activities of facilitators operating in the state and the violent acts committed against immigrants in transit, analysis of the data demonstrates that the law's implementation has actually limited the expedited access to justice of actual and potential victims. This is particularly evident in Maricopa County, where since 2006 over 1600 undocumented immigrants in transit have been charged with conspiracy to commit human smuggling (their own) at a much higher rate than the actual facilitators of their journeys.

This chapter is an analysis of violence within the local smuggling market. Just as in prior chapters, it relies on immigrants' and facilitators' accounts to map its causes, development and dynamics. While evidence suggests the structure of smuggling organizations is effective at facilitating the safe and uneventful transit of immigrants—notwithstanding its precariousness—reports of an inherently violent smuggling market in Arizona seem to bring into question the ability of smugglers to provide protection to their customers. To understand the *conditions* that generate violence (some of which can be internal to smuggling organizations, between organizations or involve state actors) and the *structures* that are in place and that allow for its consolidation, I rely on cases of smuggling-related violence present in the sample. Particular attention is given to the kidnapping phenomenon, the alleged increase of which in the Phoenix area in the 2000s had, until very recently, been attributed to the actions of smuggling facilitators. A second aspect examined is the role of structural violence, placing an emphasis on its likely and actual victims, the impact on the smuggling market and the role law enforcement plays in its expansion.

Violence and "illicit" markets

To talk about a criminalized activity's market and the use of violence is "both illuminating and misleading" (Williams 2009, 323). While identifying violent acts associated with an illicit activity like human smuggling provides an understanding of the business and the organizations that operate within it, this tactic can also result in over-generalizations and lead to erroneous conclusions.

Rather than associating a specific criminal act with a particular illicit market, the market must be understood as embedded within a broader political and ideological context. This way, the violence related to a specific market or activity appears as a response to the much larger political, social and cultural context in which a criminalized organization is operating and, to a much lesser degree, to the characteristics of the organization itself (Williams 2009, 324).

The analysis of the narratives of men and women impacted by human smuggling violence suggests that the broader context in which human smuggling takes place (i.e., immigration enforcement and control) is more critical for understanding violence than the individual violent acts associated with it.

From a criminological perspective, violence is latent and often manifest in criminalized activities. But despite being commonly described as a defining feature (Andreas and Wallman 2009, 25), violence is not an inherent element of all illicit activities (Reuter 2009; Williams 2009). Furthermore, not all illicit markets show the same degree of violence. Some markets—like drug trafficking, for example— may be more violent than others (Reuter 2009). When present, the roles of competition and turf may also play a role in the way violence is used by a specific group involved in a criminalized activity to establish markets and/or territories.

In most underground or illicit markets, violence is used as a tool to advance economic and social interests (Naylor 2009, 231) and as a method of enforcement or coercion given illicit markets' lack of access to legal recourse. Since most illicit activities take place out of the protection of court systems or regulations, their rules are socially enforced, leaving the use of violence or coercion for very unique or extreme circumstances.

In the case of smuggling, being a community-based activity, the most common form of coercion is the threat of being cut off from a group after losing the trust of other members of the group. Smuggling participants who do not comply with their part of the transit agreement are more likely to endure—and fear—social sanctions than violence. Smuggling facilitators who mistreat, cheat or hurt their customers are likely to be reported to the community as unreliable, which has a serious impact on the ability of a facilitator to carry out business, but also complicates his/her everyday life. Non-paying customers can be blacklisted and future requests for services denied.

While illegality itself is insufficient to generate high levels of violence in a market (Reuter 2009, 276), the media has characterized the smuggling market as inherently violent—or, as the Arizona Attorney General stated during a press conference, as constituting "an army of greedy, amoral, young Mexican males [who] have become a subculture unto themselves: extremely violent, extremely dangerous, all manner of bad behavior" (Wagner 2006). These characterizations have been primarily based on the most extreme examples of smuggling violence, which given their graphic nature have been effective at shaping the public's perceptions of smuggling. However, a closer look at the structure of smuggling operations raises questions over the alleged utilitarian use of violence and the inherently dangerous nature of the market.

Violence and the social organization of immigrant smuggling

Given its reliance on friendship and kinship ties and on the existence of verbal agreements, human smuggling activities are pretty self-contained to groups of people known to each other. This not only prevents the incursion of strangers who could inflict damage upon customers or put activities at risk, but also hinders the development of conflict or its escalation into violence, as data in this sample indicate. Smuggling's lack of turf and virtual absence of hierarchies also limit the causes that generate division or even lead to ruptures among members. This is not to suggest that conflict is impossible or unlikely to arise, as explained in Chapter 4. But in an activity like human smuggling where money-making opportunities depend on facilitators' access to a social network, personal differences are more likely to be put aside to avoid disruptions and detection, with members generally cooperating with one another.

Perhaps due to the nature of the ties among smuggling facilitators and the sporadic nature of their collective, smuggling-related interactions, personal conflicts among members do not seem to constitute a threat to the market. Given that facilitators must reach out to others when in need of assistance, common courtesy is typically extended to and expected from all parties whose support is sought and received. Most operations are conducted over the phone, given the varied geographical location of facilitators. Since face-to-face meetings involving all parties are unlikely to take place, facilitators develop their working collaborations by frequently spending inordinate amounts of time talking to each other over the phone. Many times, the issues discussed are completely unrelated to the actual operation. Men and women may share tips about child-rearing in the same way they discuss how to deal with non-paying customers.

Data show that facilitators who collaborate on a more constant basis, live closer to each other or spend more time together (like in the case of family members) are more likely to have disagreements. This kind of conflict is typically centered on the division of household and business responsibilities. References to domestic altercations among heterosexual couples (husbands and wives, boyfriends and girlfriends) were abundant. Women report having been subjected to domestic assaults, being involved in arguments with their husbands or other female relatives over their children's education or the degree of cleanliness in a house, or dealing with their partners' infidelities. Men also complain about women's treatment of their children, their bouts of jealousy or their excessive interest in the business's activities. However, business collaborations seemed to take precedence over family violence, conjugal tensions and even divorces. Members consistently put aside their differences once payments were sorted out and new business opportunities arose.

The horizontal, non-hierarchical structure of human smuggling operations documented here may also explain the absence of struggles over leadership or control of market segments. This however could be a limitation of the study since the testimonies obtained are only the experiences of facilitators operating as independent service providers loosely associated into groups, and no other significant form of social organization was identified in these cases. Smuggling's horizontal structure also means organizational upward mobility is not an option for facilitators, virtually eliminating the need for violence to secure a position of higher power or leadership. However, mobility does not seem to be much of a concern among facilitators, since most of them enjoy the ability to work on their own and make their own decisions without having to depend on a centralized power.

Since facilitators collaborate with one another through referrals, sharing resources and information and providing opportunities for collaboration, there is no evidence of competition or fights over turf. Furthermore, the very community-based nature of smuggling operations ensures the existence and the availability of multiple collaborative opportunities over time. In the event that a facilitator is unable to assist with one operation, there may be others in the future, or other groups he or she can assist.

If anything, a facilitator's reputation—good or bad—may be one of the few causes of serious conflict in smuggling. The likelihood of developing lasting collaborations is dependent on facilitators' work ethics. If a facilitator fails to deliver or to perform as expected, he or she may simply be cut from the group temporarily or no longer be asked to collaborate in its activities. Reasons behind the occasional arguments among facilitators may include the loss of fees or customers, the detection of an operation by law enforcement, a facilitator's arrest, failure to receive or deliver payments, etc. Yet no reprisals or revenges resulting from an operation were documented or reported.

Aside from arguments, misunderstandings and occasional bouts of anger, violence among facilitators did not seem to be a concern among the men and women in this sample. This is not to suggest that all smuggling markets are alike. Future studies into smuggling operations with different organizational structures may uncover the existence of competition, high levels of internal conflict and in-group displays of violence. But the Phoenix smuggling market, which was considered to be the largest center for smuggling operations in the US by 2010, does not appear to be characterized by any of these factors on the basis of these data alone. If one only had to consider the high effectiveness of its horizontal structure, the absence of leadership and the community-based nature of securing business for its members, one would conclude that the market is highly unlikely to undergo a transformation so radical to the point where violence among smuggling facilitators becomes a concern. Yet specific forms of violence are present in smuggling and have in fact increased the visibility of the Arizona smuggling market.

Facilitator–client interactions: threats as violence-prevention mechanisms

The interactions between smuggling facilitators and their clients, despite the existence of verbal agreements or social ties, are not always cordial. While the records show most journeys are uneventful, misunderstandings or arguments (typically involving finances) are common. The majority of the conflicts reported between facilitators and their clients involve unexpected changes to the terms of the initial agreement, particularly through an unannounced increase of fees.

In general, most smuggling agreements include all the costs involved with a customer's transit from a departure point (usually a location along the border) to a final in-country destination. Upon arrival to his or her final destination, the customer contacts friends or family to inform them of his or her status and asks them to pay for any additional fees that may be owed to the facilitator. Once the fees have been received and verified by a specific facilitator, the agreement is considered fulfilled. There are no more obligations between the parties.

The sample included several reports of immigrants who were informed upon arrival to the Phoenix area that they had to pay additional fees in order to be taken to their final destination.[1] While it could appear as if border crossers had no recourse other than to accept the terms established by the facilitator, the changes always generated protests. People opposed the new fees and refused to make additional payments, objecting to what they characterized as "an abuse." While people eventually pay the fees, verbal and physical altercations do ensue.

One of these incidents involved the escalation of an argument between a woman and her facilitator. While traveling with her husband, the woman challenged the coordinator's decision to charge them an additional US$1000 per person to take them to New York City, which was their final destination. After calling the coordinator a *ratero* (petty thief) in front of all the clients, the woman informed him she would not pay. A police report describes the facts:

> [There was] one incident where the boss of the house got into an argument with a husband and a wife over the increased smuggling fee. Originally, the couple was to be [sic] $2500 a piece. When they arrived at the drop house, the fee was increased to $3500. The girl told the boss that he was robbing them. The two started yelling at each other and the boss told her husband to have his bitch shut up or that he would fuck her up.
>
> (Maricopa County v. Chacon Perez 2009, 3)

A second witness confirmed how:

> the boss got mad at the girl because she complained about the price, and so he took his gun out, racked a round into the chamber and told her husband to calm her down or he would beat the crap out of her.
>
> (Maricopa County v. Chacon Perez 2009, 3)

The terrified husband reprimanded his wife and asked her not to say anything else. But the witnesses also went on to state that the "boss" did help the couple get in contact with some of their friends, who lent them the money they needed to complete the fee. While the couple ultimately paid for their transportation in full, they were yet to be transported to their destination by the time police irrupted at the safe house. The smuggling facilitators were arrested, but the customers—including the couple—were also charged for their participation in what was alleged to be a human smuggling conspiracy. The money paid was confiscated as part of the investigation and was never returned to the couple.

While in most cases threats do not materialize, they are also used to convey enough pressure upon other migrants who may be present at the safe house to urge their families and friends to pay off any fees that may be pending or due. Once balances are covered, migrants in transit are taken to their destination or relatives are asked to pick them up at a specific location (usually a public place like a parking lot or shopping center). In these specific cases, there were no reports of immigrants having been physically harmed.

Smuggling facilitators dislike having to contact families about overdue or unpaid balances. They find the extra work tiresome and unnecessary, alleging verbal agreements like those regulating migrants' transits are serious affairs and not meant to be broken:

> So that time after we counted the people and straightened out the accounts I once again came short. Yeah, something like $400. I didn't [add up the fees] right. And you know why this happened? Because I am a good person. Because I tell [customers]: yeah, sure, go ahead, pay me later, when you get a job, and what happens? That they freaking avoid me afterwards! I think people take advantage of you because you are nice to them. That is why I don't want to do this anymore sometimes, because I am tired of being taken advantage of.
>
> (Maricopa County v. Robaina 2006, Affidavit, 20)

This conversation reveals the disappointment of the facilitator when informed that one of his clients had left without paying most of his smuggling fee—US$1350. The financial mishap also meant that the facilitator was unable to cover the rent for the safe house, which would result in the loss of some business as he did not have a place available to house customers, having to pass the business on to another facilitator.

Most facilitators seem to simply absorb the losses, as the last example shows (the non-paying customer is sent back to the coordinator or recruiter who arranged for his travel to a point along the border, or is simply let go without payment after a few days). Other groups may continue pushing for payment through negotiation calls to family and relatives. Facilitators do grant, subjectively, "reasonable" periods of time of a few days for relatives to come up with the balance. If there is further hesitation on the families' part or if payment is delayed for several days without a valid explanation, the facilitator may turn to more serious threats to "encourage" prompt payment.

The increased threat strategy, however, is a delicate matter, the negotiation of which requires tact and patience—virtues lacked by many facilitators. Whenever facilitators relied on threats, these usually backfired. In all cases, the terrified family members opted for reaching out to police instead of continuing to negotiate with the caller, even when the arrest of the facilitator involved the arrest and deportation of the client as well and the loss of any fees already paid.

The outcome of these cases suggests that it is in the facilitators' interest, rather that the clients' to provide as many conveniences as possible for the fulfillment of the financial part of the agreements in order to avoid conflict or detection. Facilitators are not part of established organizations that provide them with training on how to be patient or deal with difficult, obnoxious or simply non-paying customers. But the key to reducing the risk of detection is to work with customers to avoid disruptions and inconveniences. Unfortunately, by the time police respond to calls, the conflict has reached a point of no return and there are unwanted consequences—primarily of a legal nature—for both facilitators and their clients.

Despite the occurrence of agitated arguments, ominous threats and occasional shoving matches (which are not unique to illicit markets), there are no indications of escalated violence among smuggling facilitators and the clients who travel with their assistance. The existence of a preceding agreement among the parties and the referral-based nature of the smuggling market tend to work in the customer's favor. Customers can ultimately refuse to pay their balances, or in the worst of cases—as we have seen—report the facilitator's behavior to police or to potential customers, either way severely impacting the facilitator's ability to conduct future business.

Constructing victimizers

Despite the disagreements and tension between smuggling facilitators, and also between facilitators and their clients, conflict is generally contained before escalating into full-blown acts of violence. And yet Arizona's human smuggling market tends to be portrayed as the most violent in the nation. Reports of undocumented immigrants being kidnapped at gunpoint by sadistic Mexican gangs of human smugglers continue to make headlines. Frequent stories of dozens of undocumented immigrants held against their will by coyotes in rundown houses throughout the Phoenix area, or of high-speed police chases along nearby freeways, generate grave concern among the public.

Violence in smuggling does take place, and it can—and has proven to—be heinous. However, it occurs only under very specific circumstances. First, and without exception, all cases involving violent acts in this sample involved immigrants who traveled without the protection of an established familial or social migration group—that is, men and women who traveled without a referral or who lacked the knowledge and/or resources necessary to inform their journeys were more likely to fall victims of violent crimes. Second, when violent acts did occur, they seem to have been executed by groups that did not operate as traditional smuggling groups do. These "bad actors," as they are defined in criminology, were small groups consisting almost entirely of men, which engaged in the commission of multiple illicit activities aside from holding undocumented immigrants against their will for ransom (from drug trafficking to home invasions to armed robbery).

The kidnapping, extortion and even sexual and physical assaults many undocumented immigrants in transit are unfortunate to experience do not seem to be the act of smuggling facilitators like those identified in this study. Instead, these acts are carried out by groups with virtually no experience in smuggling, although some of those arrested due to their involvement in the commission of violent acts reported having been at some point in contact with a smuggling group, or even having relied on its services. Contrary to smuggling facilitators, the effectiveness of these groups, and their recognition, relies on the degree of violence they display. While these groups, like smuggling facilitators, also rely on placing calls to immigrants' families to collect fees through banks or wire services, their similarities end there. And yet the modus operandi of these groups has been equated to that of smuggling facilitators, and law enforcement refers to both groups, regardless of the existence of these essential differences, as smuggling crews. Assuming smuggling facilitator activities are equal to those carried out by other groups who are not in the business of smuggling, and then explaining both groups' actions as violent acts of rivalry and competition does not merely raise questions regarding law enforcement's understanding of smuggling's dynamics. It may also play a role in law enforcement's ability to respond to violent acts related to smuggling, which may result in the victimization of immigrants in transit. Law enforcement, by operating on the basis of over-generalizations, may actually be contributing to the violence that has afflicted the market.

Defining "bajadores"

The smuggling violence that has captured the public's imagination has been explained by media, local politicians and law enforcement as a sign of growing conflicts in the division of what is often characterized as a highly profitable market among competing transnational smuggling organizations. The characterization of the local smuggling market as highly profitable, or as impacted by competition or dominated by criminal organizations, reflects the limited knowledge and understanding of the dynamics of smuggling operations on the part of law enforcement and policy makers alike (or their unwillingness to understand them). But what is most troubling is that this stance makes the identification of new actors, trends or threats virtually impossible, which in turn impacts the effectiveness of law enforcement efforts, and further exposes undocumented immigrants to violence and victimization.

The incursions so widely reported by the media are not the reflection of competition or rivalry among human smuggling groups. Their presence suggests the existence of an altogether different form of organized activity that, unlike smuggling, relies on violence to achieve its goals. These newer groups do not operate as part of extended families or acquaintances: rather, they are constituted by groups of 4–8 men who engage in opportunistic crime involving targets likely to produce fast cash returns—home invasions, burglaries, armed robberies, stealing of drugs or drug profits. Given the prevalence of human smuggling activities in the state, these groups have also been known to target smuggling facilitators, although not for cash. Instead, these groups steal or kidnap undocumented immigrants in transit from their facilitators to then demand ransoms for their release:

> Adolfo went on to explain he, El Guero, Papayo, Mister U and Pariente were not smugglers but *"bajadores."* They would rob drug dealers and human smugglers in order to make money. Adolfo explained how he has been without work and has had difficulty surviving which led him to do this. Adolfo met Papayo and started working. Adolfo described where the group went and kidnapped the illegals from a drop house and removed some televisions [. . .]. The televisions were transported back to the house where they had split the money they charged to the families of the immigrants. They used a Honda which was stolen from the house as well. Adolfo told me about a drug robbery [. . .]. Adolfo, Daniel, Carlos and other unidentified subjects robbed three Sinaloan men of approximately one gram of methamphetamine. Adolfo said they went in through the front door [. . .]. The drugs were sold and they split the money. Adolfo received $300 for his involvement.
>
> (Maricopa County v. Alfaro–Martinez, 2008)

Known in underground markets as *bajadores*—"unloaders" in Spanish—the activities of these crews have been known to members of underground markets for decades, although their existence was only recognized by American law enforcement recently. References to the activities of *bajadores* are common in folk songs and oral traditions along the border. Groups of *bajadores* are described as low-class, unskilled, amateur robbers who steal cargo from more professional, more organized groups of individuals involved in the transportation of illicit goods. The term *bajador* was initially designated to refer to crews that would take drug cargo from its "lawful" owners at gunpoint. The term has since been adapted—and adopted—to refer to the men who opportunistically take immigrants in transit by force from the groups that facilitate their journeys. The term was only until recently discovered by media and law enforcement in the context of the activities involving the kidnapping by force of undocumented immigrants.

In this study, participants described how *bajadores* operated in three different ways: by irrupting while heavily armed into safe houses—usually at nighttime – kidnapping undocumented immigrants, many times breaking up large groups of immigrants into smaller ones to facilitate their transportation. They were also known to scout local routes from where they could take migrants in transit by force. And in one instance, *bajadores* paid a member of a smuggling facilitator group for information to locate a group of undocumented immigrants about to pay their smuggling fees and whose families would be likely to have immediate access to pay a ransom on demand.

Once a group of undocumented immigrants is kidnapped or taken by force, *bajadores* take them to a location where they are kept against their will. The *bajadores* place a ransom call demanding immediate payment to release the migrant. Families are warned against contacting the authorities. In *bajador*-related cases, all victims were consistently subjected to some degree of emotional, physical or sexual violence, ranging from being pushed around and threatened, to enduring beatings, electric shocks and even sexual assaults.

While *bajador* activities are typically described by law enforcement as a variation of human smuggling, the degree of visibility in which *bajadores* engage – shootings in heavily populated neighborhoods, midday assaults or break-ins, chases along local freeways—is further proof that their modus operandi is unlike that of smuggling organizations, which work at reducing their visibility, minimizing potential interactions with authorities and avoiding engagement in any other activity that could compromise a smuggling operation.

Bajadores may also have shorter career spans than those of smuggling facilitators, mostly due to their visibility. Their excessive tendency to display violence generates unwanted attention, making them more exposed to detection by law enforcement. Given this reliance on violent tactics, *bajadores* are also much more likely than smuggling facilitators to be reported to the police by abused or tortured immigrants and their families, who in this sample contacted the authorities to report the offense almost immediately after the placing of the ransom call.

Another characteristic common to *bajadores* is the high use of illicit substances compared to that of smuggling facilitators, who reported no drug use or only recreational levels of drug use. Reliance on cocaine and methamphetamine is reportedly extensive among *bajador* crews, as they ingest the substances in order to stay awake to watch their hostages around the clock. The use of substances creates dangerous conditions for hostages: multiple assaults took place while *bajadores* were under the influence of drugs.

In summary, unlike the case of the majority of smuggling operators, who collaborate as part of a loosely formed group of independent service providers, *bajadores* seem to be assembled to carry out multiple forms of illicit activity, one of which may involve the kidnapping of undocumented immigrants from their smugglers. *Bajadores* also demonstrate a clear reliance on violence and weapons, and self-report higher levels of drug use and dependency.

From victims to victimizers

According to testimonies of victims of kidnapping cases, many *bajador* groups force the immigrants they hold captive to assist them in their activities when they are unable to pay off ransom fees. In a fashion similar to the hiring of clients as facilitators, clients are told that in exchange for their safe release they will have to perform duties as assigned (house cleaning, cooking, acting as guards, etc.).

In a hard-to-explain twist, several migrants who initially collaborated out of fear or who did so reluctantly reportedly became full-blown collaborators of the *bajador* group, going as far as committing violent acts against other kidnapped immigrants. When arrested and questioned, multiple men admit they took the side of the *bajador* group when they were unable to pay their fees. Most of them deny having inflicted violence against other migrants, despite evidence to the contrary.

On August 27, 2009, police responded to a 911 call at a drop house in Maricopa County's West Valley. Locked inside the house, police found 11 kidnapping victims, including the person who made the call, and three kidnapping suspects. Police also found wooden dowel rods that had been used to beat the victims, as well as loaded weapons and cell phones. The room where the victims were held was boarded up with plywood to avoid escape (Maricopa County v. Garcia–Medina, 2007).

According to in-court testimonies, two guards would constantly point their handguns at the victims in a threatening manner, while a third man made extortion phone calls to collect ransoms. When Antonio Hernandez, along with another immigrant, tried to make a run for the door, a guard responsible for preventing escapes stopped both men before beating them with the closet rod.

Hernandez described how a man would administer electric shocks to hostages in the house's bathroom. He also disclosed that electric probes were put under his arms when the ransom his family had promised to wire was not ready for pick up at a nearby wire transfer store. Later on, while under the influence of cocaine, the *bajadores* used a pair of electric shears to shave off his hair (Maricopa County v. Garcia-Medina 2007, Findings, 289).

Men who collaborate with the *bajador* groups (only one case involved a woman) reportedly threaten migrants, deprive them of food or water, deny them access to restroom facilities and carry weapons with the sole purpose of causing intimidation, etc. More extreme cases in this sample involved serious beatings and several incidents of sexual violence and victimization. Contrary to the assumption that women are the most frequent targets of sexual violence in smuggling, only one first-hand account of male-on-female sexual assault was found in this sample. The rest involved acts of male-on-male sexual violence. While the most common acts of this nature involve sexual humiliation, the record included reports of male immigrants being forced to perform sexual acts on each other or on their captors, and of victimizers administering electric shocks to victims' genital areas.

The risks of conceptualizing smuggling as inherently violent

The evidence suggests that the most extreme acts of violence in smuggling are not necessarily performed by smuggler facilitators themselves, who in the worst of circumstances may simply have little recourse aside from threats to enforce compliance, cooperation or payment from their customers. Kidnapping, physical and sexual assaults, and other acts of physical or emotional torture present in this sample seem instead to be primarily the acts of *bajador* crews, in addition to those of immigrants in transit who appear to collaborate with *bajadores* and victimize other immigrants like themselves (a quite frequent and no less problematic form of smuggling violence).

Despite the alleged risks human smuggling organizations pose to local public safety, smuggling enforcement efforts have shown scant interest in understanding their dynamics. Instead, based on police reports present in the sample, law enforcement responses to the activities of smuggling and *bajador* crews are virtually identical. This approach to smuggling enforcement and the similar treatment given to facilitators and *bajadores* by the court system should not come as a surprise. It echoes the state's posture in defining smuggling crimes, which through the implementation of the anti-human smuggling statute, or the Coyote Law, has indicted smuggling facilitators as well as the immigrants they transport, charging both parties with the commission of human smuggling acts.

Undermining definitions

The broad definition of smuggling, the imprecision to identify its actors and the tendency to approach the market as inherently violent have resulted in the labeling of all incidents involving contact between smuggling facilitators, *bajador* crews and undocumented immigrants, regardless of their nature, as violent—despite the wide range of contexts and actors involved. The rampant success of the Maricopa County Attorney in prosecuting smuggling activity in Maricopa County was in fact dependent on these very vague approaches to smuggling activity.

An offense for which designation has also generated a certain degree of controversy has been smuggling-related kidnapping. In Maricopa County, acts as varied as the taking of undocumented immigrants by force by *bajador* crews from smuggling facilitators, police responses to 911 calls to report an immigrant's inability to pay off fees owed to a smuggling facilitator, ransom calls placed by immigrant victims and/or *bajador* crews and calls to police responding to immigrant escapes from safe house incidents have resulted in the filing of kidnapping charges against *bajadores*, smuggling facilitators and even immigrants in transit.

The holding of undocumented immigrants in transit by smuggling organizations can strictly be the result of the waiting period between an immigrant's arrival to his or her destination and his or her family's ability to allocate the necessary resources to liquidate smuggling payments and associated fees. Frequently, immigrants and/or their families miscalculate their ability to pay; in which case, as a sign of good faith, an immigrant remains by the side or in close contact with the coordinator until the debt has been liquidated. This is not to dismiss the cases in which, even after the payments have been fulfilled, smuggling organizations alter the terms of the original transit agreement. Or the tragic instances when immigrants face abuse, even torture at the hands of *bajadores*.

But the state's tendency to rely on over-generalized, blanket designations of what constitutes an offense in order to prosecute immigrant-related crimes is problematic. The measure does not merely impact the lives of facilitators, *bajadores* or other parties who may be part of undocumented immigrants' victimization, but it may also be placing immigrants in increased danger. Law enforcement SWAT team-like responses put immigrants at risk of sustaining injury in situations where no actual violence has taken place. Police incursions frequently lead to the loss of immigrants' fees or investment, creating immense pressures among the friends or families who have incurred debts to finance the journey through high-interest loans (Kyle and Dale 2001). What is perhaps most troubling in terms of legal implications is the tendency to label a wide range of criminal activities as smuggling events, which has actually undermined the very concept of the offense, as we have seen in the conviction of undocumented immigrants charged with conspiring to commit their own smuggling.

A similar transformation has taken place in the case of kidnapping offenses, the prevalence of which was, until recently, believed to be connected to the activities of smuggling facilitators, and which earned Phoenix the dubious title of "Kidnapping Capital of the US."[2]

Challenging the violence argument: the case of Phoenix's kidnapping statistics

According to data provided by the Phoenix Police Department, kidnapping reports in the Phoenix area, as shown in Table 6.1, had been on the rise since the early 2000s, when they went from 113 in 2000 to 317 in 2009, peaking at 358 in 2008.

The numbers do in fact show an increase in the number of kidnappings reported over the past decade. Phoenix Police Department rushed to attribute the increase to the growing presence and influence of drug and human smuggling groups in the city—this despite the fact that crime levels in Phoenix were at their lowest in decades (FBI 2011). The abundance of media coverage involving smuggling activity seemed to confirm those asseverations, and so neither the numbers provided by

Table 6.1 Departmental reports for kidnapping, Phoenix Police Department, Arizona (January 1, 2000 to December 31, 2009)*

Year	Kidnapping incidents	Kidnapping incidents—information only	Total
2000	96	17	113
2001	116	25	141
2002	161	39	200
2003	189	48	237
2004	178	51	229
2005	173	55	228
2006	190	41	231
2007	260	84	344
2008	299	59	358
2009	265	52	317

Data Source: Phoenix Police Department, Crime Analysis and Research Unit, February 2010

Note

*The totals include all incidents listed as kidnappings that were assigned to the Home Invasion Kidnapping Enforcement (HIKE) squads and Violent Crimes

Bureau Robbery (VCBR) squads in order to demonstrate the total number of cases reported during the stated time period. It is important to note, however, that incidents marked as "information only" may not contain enough detail and these should be excluded from the overall count of kidnapping incidents.

police or their nature were ever brought into question. Furthermore, the sudden appearance of the *bajador* phenomenon seemed to confirm police's claims that kidnappings were most likely related to smuggling activity. The political pressure to support anti-immigrant measures, as well as the aggressive enforcement carried out by other law enforcement agencies and which targeted undocumented immigrants did also allow for the numbers to remain unchallenged.

Through my experience as both a family court associate and a presentence investigator, I knew that the majority of kidnapping acts that were reported to police typically involved domestic violence or custodial interference cases—that is, the removal by force of a child or children by a non-custodial parent. The apparent and rapid transformation of kidnapping from a family-based crime to one dominating the city's crime statistics simply failed to make sense.

During the data collection period of this project, I reached out to the research unit of the Phoenix Police Department and requested kidnapping numbers to explore its alleged correlation to the smuggling market structure and operations. It was then that I first noticed that the statistics being compiled by police made no distinctions in the nature of the kidnappings reported, making it impossible to determine on the basis of the numbers alone if the increase was indeed related to the activities of human smugglers or if it was linked to any other crimes or activities—including parental kidnappings or abductions. Furthermore, the Phoenix Police Department's decision to include home invasions as part of kidnapping numbers—as well as the incorporation of multiple offenses that, under regular circumstances, would have not been reported as kidnappings (see Table 6.1 note)—suggested a new interpretation on the part of the department of what constituted kidnapping.

Having approached the Phoenix Police Department's research unit to express my concern, I was informed that Phoenix Police was not obligated to keep track of kidnappings by their nature, or to specify the rationale behind the inclusion of offenses as home invasions into kidnapping statistics. A formal request for a breakdown of the kinds of kidnappings being used to calculate the city's totals was denied on the grounds that that kind of data reporting was not available as public record. Phoenix Police replied:

> The existing reports that we have for kidnappings just show count by month or count by year but do not break the kidnappings into any further detail, so [there is no] breakdown of kidnappings by race or by whether they are related to undocumented immigrants and human and drug trafficking/smuggling, etc. To get at the information we would have to build a custom query and complete some additional analysis, and [such] information is not considered information that is available under public records law.
>
> (Schick 2010)

In late January of 2011, allegations that Phoenix Police had manipulated kidnapping numbers for most of the past decade in order to secure federal grants emerged (Hermann 2011). The scandal led to the resignation of the Phoenix Police

Chief—and to claims that he was being unfairly punished for his refusal to support the implementation of SB1070 in the state (Bui and Hermann 2011). Regardless of the reason behind the handling of the numbers, the lack of criteria explaining the decision to designate multiple and different crimes as kidnapping incidents should not have led to the conclusion that the growth of kidnapping activity in the City of Phoenix could be entirely attributed to the activities of human smuggling facilitators alone.

The state's efforts to conceptualize kidnapping as an element of smuggling show the troubling implications of approaching an activity as complex as human smuggling only from a criminalized stance. The narratives of both immigrants and facilitators provide critical evidence of the kinds of activities to the interior of smuggling networks and of the role of violence in the market. Improved responses to the smuggling phenomenon require a closer look at its social dynamics, leaving aside the emphasis on identifying criminal behaviors, and instead examining the social context in which the market develops and takes place.

Conclusions

> *I was just an accomplice.*[3]

On April 6, 2009, Pedro Armenta-Campoy was arrested during a SWAT team operation to rescue Rodrigo Garcia, who had been kidnapped by a group of *bajadores* who demanded a US$2000 ransom in exchange for his release. According to Garcia, Armenta-Campoy had tied his hands and feet to a chair and threatened to cut off his fingers if the ransom wasn't paid (Maricopa County v. Armenta–Campoy, 2009, p. 1).

Armenta-Campoy was charged with one count of kidnapping and sentenced to five years in prison. Garcia, despite being a victim in the case, was not afforded the protections given to victims of violent crime. Following his rescue, he was instead released to the immigration service, which deported him back to Mexico, his country of origin. Garcia's input was not considered during the sentencing of any of the *bajadores* involved in the case. The victim advocate assigned to his case made no attempts to locate him, and the court investigator in charge of completing the sentencing recommendations in the case did not even include his name in the report.

Conflict and the potential for violence do exist in smuggling operations. As I have noted, many migrants whose travel agreements are changed by their smuggling operators opt for paying higher fees or accepting other financial agreements that will most likely impact their finances in order to avoid potential disagreements. These changes are not merely accepted: arguments do arise, but threats or fear of violence usually mean the end of any financial dispute. Smuggling operators, especially those with limited experience, have a hard time dealing with financial losses, family conflicts and problematic customers. But violence does not seem to be an inherent characteristic of the business when it is run by traditional, community-based groups.

And yet violence does take place. Reports of smuggling-related violence in Phoenix have been on the rise, but reliable statistics are hard to come by. The reports may be the result of increased public awareness, more intensive enforcement or the growing visibility of crews of *bajadores* or even smuggling facilitators. But as the case of the Phoenix Police Department and manipulating statistics suggests, there has not been a clear interest on the part of law enforcement to understand the dynamics of smuggling, and instead its visibility has been used to advance political and financial goals while all along reinscribing racialized and xenophobic images of smuggling facilitators as criminal predators.

The state, by purposely defining acts like smuggling or kidnapping in broad terms, may be causing a greater level of victimization than that generated by the actions of smuggling facilitators or *bajadores*. Relying on excessive enforcement and massive prosecution practices, Maricopa County convicted over 1600 irregular migrants by charging them with conspiring to commit their own smuggling – an event that did not involve the commission of any violent acts but yet resulted in the incarceration and prosecution of thousands of non-dangerous individuals.

This assessment is not an attempt to under-estimate the work of law enforcement to prevent criminal activity. Yet it shows that the range of forms of violence or aggression irregular migrants, extralegal border crossers and their families are likely to face as a result of an extralegal border crossing do not come from smuggling facilitators or *bajadores* alone. It is also correlated to the state's immigration enforcement practices, which are not aimed at rescuing potential victims of violent acts. These action reflect local state and federal authorities' efforts to increase immigration enforcement activities and numbers in urban and rural communities across the nation. They are also powerful reminders of the second-class citizenship communities of color—in this case, US citizens of Latino origin—are likely to encounter in their dealings with the law (Romero and Serag 2005). Citing national security concerns, local immigration enforcement in the US has come to rely upon the use of excessive displays of force—aggressive incursions, displays of heavy weaponry, unjustified forceful entry—all practices not too different from the acts of violence in which some smuggling facilitators partake.

In order to avoid law enforcement-initiated disruptions, smuggling facilitators are forced to further hide their activities, to opt for more extreme routes to avoid detection, to demand greater discretion from their customers, etc. These demands in turn create tensions on the inside of the smuggling groups that, even in a market like smuggling, which generally lacks competition or turf, can lead to ruptures, fights and regional conflicts, modifying ties or even destroying the collaboration that once made operations successful and sustainable. These conflicts, and their effects—which do include the exercise of violent acts—are counterproductive for business and may be at the center of the transformation of the human smuggling market, which at a time was known for its ability to provide safe transits. But most importantly, contention among actors (including law enforcement officers, human smuggling facilitators, *bajadores* and border crossers themselves) creates increasingly vulnerable conditions for those who rely on the provision of smuggling services for their transit.

Most of the smuggling-related cases that generate media attention are those involving extreme episodes of abuse or death: the all-too-frequent narratives of migrants dying in the desert, suffocating in trailers, drowning while crossing bodies of water (Andreas and Wallman 2009, 227; Zhang 2007; Kyle and Scarcelli 2009). But the actions of law enforcement that lead smuggling facilitators and immigrants to opt for more dangerous practices during their journeys, and the policies that continue to punish those unable to fulfill the state's restrictive immigration requirements, are distant from being designated as criminal or conducive of victimization outside of academic or NGO circles. They are not considered a form of violence by the state, nor are its implications considered graphic enough to deserve media attention or reporting, as if those actions played no part in the continuum of violence that extralegal border crossers and asylum seekers face.

Notes

1 This situation is not unique to smuggling operations along the US–Mexico border. Zhang (2008) documented that the practice of ramping up prices is commonplace among Chinese human smugglers.
2 For examples of media coverage on kidnappings and violence, see Myers (2010), Randall (2009) and Johnson (2009).
3 Maricopa County v. Armenta Campoy, CR2009–123885–001DT

Conclusions
Smuggling in the era of security

Poets and beggars, musicians and prophets, warriors and scoundrels, all creatures of that unbridled reality, we had to ask but little to the imagination, because the biggest challenge for us has been the lack of conventional means to render our lives believable. This, my friends, is the crux of our solitude.

(Gabriel Garcia Marquez 1982, *The Solitude of Latin America*)

A few years ago, driving home after leaving one of Maricopa County's jails, I thought about the events of the day. I had just spent most of my Saturday afternoon sitting on the floor of a detention cell, talking to a smuggling facilitator believed to be the head of a large organization responsible for the transportation of hundreds of irregular immigrants across the Arizona desert. I don't remember what his name was, only that at 26 he was not much older than I was at the time. We had identical musical tastes, liked the same brand of beer—and our families were from the same state in Mexico.

After several hours of great conversation, I realized it was time to say goodbye. I packed my notes and I walked out of the security area to leave the interview room. Suddenly, the young man ran to the door as if he had forgotten to say something important and yelled through the metal bars of the cell, waking up the sheriff's officer dozing off by the door: "If you ever have a friend or a relative who needs to get through, look me up! I'll get them across for free!"

It was not the first time that I had been honored with such a gracious offer. During my time as an interviewer in Maricopa County, I spent vast amounts of time talking to the men and women about to be sentenced for their participation in smuggling. We would talk about family, relationships, friends, travels; I would share with them some of the daily news, or even some tabloid gossip. But most importantly, we laughed—we laughed at how the realities of smuggling seemed so surreal that people would think we had imagined them. Or perhaps because we knew what Gabriel Garcia Marquez meant when he addressed the audience that had come to see him receive the Nobel Prize: *Because the biggest challenge for us was the lack of conventional means to render our lives believable.*

That day, following my conversation with the young man, I began to wonder about my future. I had been conducting interviews for several years. People had been sharing with me their hopes, their fears, their frustrations. What was I doing with them? I was growing weary of completing those thick brown files full of incriminatory statements that described smuggling facilitators as hei-nous criminals, as violent predators scouting Phoenix's freeways for victims. What was next? I had never had a more fulfilling job. But what was my com-mitment to those who I interviewed? What did I want to do with their voices, and why?

As I write the concluding paragraphs of this study, I wonder if I have even vaguely described the compassion, the courage, the hard work and the determina-tion present in each one of the narratives of the men and women whose voices were included in this study. I wonder if, while reading these pages, the guides, the walkers, the coordinators or drivers of Maricopa County would recognize them-selves. Or if the translations of their accounts are accurate reflections of their thoughts, their feelings of anger, despair, hope. And it saddens me to think I will never know the answer. Most of the people I spoke with were eventually deported, or moved to other states following the completion of their sentences. And despite the fact that I always made sure to leave a card, and people excitedly assured me they would call, nobody I interviewed ever contacted me.

I decided to study human smuggling operations without knowing where my research interests would take me or what I would find. I think I initially and rather naïvely believed smuggling acts as narrated by the men and women I interviewed were, if nothing else, illuminating. Exciting. I remember the looks on my cousins' faces when I'd speak about my most recent interview with a courageous female smuggler or about a meeting with a mysterious facilitator being held in the high security tower. It took me some time to understand that these narratives were much more than personal accounts of bravery or determination. I began to uncover the way criminalization processes hindered human lives, *real lives*; how they cut them short. I also discovered the scarcity of empirical research in the area. I real-ized the lack of information regarding a market that was so poorly understood was only simplifying the vilification of those who facilitated crossings, misconstrued and often dependent on xenophobic perceptions.

When law enforcement and government agencies began to show an interest in my work by funding it, I began to wonder if I could use those spaces to speak about an idea that seemed radical at the time: the possibility that smuggling activi-ties, far from being criminally organized or a threat to the stability of the nation-state, were efforts on the part of the working poor to improve the quality of their lives through the creation of alternative forms of income. But at the same time, I was also starting to think—again, rather naïvely—about the possibility that new findings, that new understandings of smuggling along borders, by privileging the voices of those the state had taught the public to fear and reject, could provide new understandings of those who lived along the margins.

My intention is not that of vindicating the role of smuggling facilitators or to transform them into supernatural, subaltern heroes. In fact I didn't have to: they had already achieved that status among the communities of immigrants whose journeys they worked hard at facilitating. But I was convinced that the current characterizations of the smuggling business were inaccurate and biased. Furthermore, immigration law enforcement operations were providing mounting evidence of how misleading definitions and understandings of the market were disproportionately affecting very specific groups in Arizona—Latino immigrant men, women and their children. And so this study became an attempt to understand the local human smuggling market from the perspectives of those who participated in it, emphasizing not the activity's criminal nature, but the social interactions that emerged among its actors and the role played by the state in imposing sanctions.

While I was encouraged by the possibilities of my research, I almost immediately became aware of its limitations. Mostly due to legal concerns, my initial methodology had to be reworked. The possibility of establishing personal contact with released smuggling facilitators was eliminated from the onset by the criminal justice agency where I intended to conduct my research. I overcame this limitation by relying instead on the first-hand accounts of smuggling facilitators available through online public files, which posed no access restrictions. I was also unable to compile a sample of the entire smuggling market in the state—I was limited to the cases that, by virtue of having been detected by law enforcement, had resulted in a conviction and were therefore available for research. Initially, the smuggling-related activities of other groups that had proven more effective at avoiding detection were not included. Something similar happened in the topic of women's participation in smuggling. I initially failed to recognize the role women played in smuggling, and it wasn't in fact until the men I interviewed began to complain about the level of domination women exerted in the market that I took a closer look at how gender was operationalized in smuggling activities. While I certainly found no evidence of this alleged takeover, the book does in fact reflect on the wide range of experiences of women in smuggling. References to women's participation in the smuggling market over the years and subsequent research in other regions do indicate women's participation in smuggling is significantly higher than what scholars and policy makers have been able to document so far. I encourage scholars to pursue that task.

I avoided expanding the scope of the research to aspects that, while interesting, would not have contributed to my analysis of the social dynamics of human smuggling operations, like drug trafficking activities. While rare, events involving drug transportation were occasionally reported by facilitators as part of their statements, mostly in reference to the transportation of drugs for personal use, and were not related to the provision of smuggling services. The only references to drugs that were relevant to an analysis of the kind I sought to provide were those involving drug use among *bajadores*. While outside of the scope of this project, it is perhaps important to highlight that no systematic ties between drug and human smuggling organizations were found in the sample, most likely because, at the most basic level (that is, logistics-wise), the likelihood of human smuggling facilitators being able to perform drug trafficking activities simultaneously is slim at best.

Another quite important aspect of this analysis involves the issue of violence. While I reiterate throughout this study that violence in smuggling is highly specific in nature, and that the smuggling market despite being illicit does not show signs of being inherently violent, violent acts against immigrants do take place. However, as I reflected in Chapter 6, a serious analysis of violence in smuggling should not be limited to studying the violent acts committed by smuggling facilitators alone – which are scarce and occur under very specific circumstances. Instead, the potential for smuggling-related violence should be understood as one, and only one, element of the continuum of violence faced by immigrants during their border crossing experiences. As I have shown, while smuggling-related violence has the potential to be heinous—as demonstrated by the attacks some immigrants are unfortunate to endure at the hands of groups like *bajadores*, for example—the state has also been a central actor in the victimization endured by immigrants in transit. This is evident in the examples involving raids, SWAT team responses and the treatment of victims as suspects, which includes the lack of recognition of their victim status and the elimination of any protections to which they would otherwise be entitled.

The characterization of smuggling facilitators as violent and callous criminals is not new, but the way their activities have been increasingly portrayed in the context of national security and border protection as threats to the nation-state is. An effective way to secure public rejection toward smuggling has been to suggest smuggling facilitators would be likely to participate in the transportation of terrorists who could carry out massive attacks against US interests (Kyle and Koslowski, 2001, p. 12). While the very definition of what constitutes a terrorist act is highly suspect, these statements are further complicated by the xenophobic perceptions surrounding the presence of Latinos in places like Arizona. Calls to limit Latino social, civic and political participation through racist legislation abound in the state and have counted on the support of a public who, amid the gradual loss of its privileges, has found, with immigrants, the perfect target of its frustrations.

In the aftermath of 9/11, governments have taken further steps to control the flows of people and goods along their borders, devising plans to improve surveillance and to increase the policing and removal of the "alien invaders." Increasing interventions by the state to stop all forms of undocumented, unauthorized transits and flows, particularly through the over-criminalization and the construction of immigrants and minorities as threats, are common in the global north. And so by being described as a highly complex, mafia-like enterprise, with ties to markets as diverse as sex trafficking and the weapons trade, with the power to transport terrorists in the same way as drugs, human smuggling groups have become the ideal and preferred target of the nation-state's criminalization efforts.

The US–Mexico border, and more recently the Arizona–Sonora corridor, has been transformed, just like many other border regions in the world, into a space of interdiction: a conflict zone where the state implements policies that seek to control actors and commodities defined as illegal (Aguiar 2010, 1). Neoliberal practices have also meant the transformation of borders in an attempt to redefine the very notions of what constitutes state and nation. Smuggling facilitators pose, in this context, a dual threat: their actions not only show the de-territorialized character of the border, but their success at promoting migration constitutes a direct challenge to the very state desperate to re-establish its diminishing powers. In this context, the criminalization of smuggling facilitators is only likely to continue—in just the same way as the need for the work of Cynthia, Mrs Quintas, Rayo and Honduras will continue to exist.

Glossary

As David Spener noticed in his research among smugglers in Texas (2009), border crossings activities—and those who are connected to them as participants or facilitators—have over time given rise to and developed a rich, complex terminology that seeks to reflect the dynamics of irregular migration. This linguistic cadre often reflects the ironies and challenges inherent to the criminalization of irregular border crossings. Furthermore, most of this rhetoric is vernacular in nature, and often includes humoristic undertones.

Ayudante Helper. Often acting as assistants to a coordinator, ayudantes assist with the day-to-day handling of smuggling activities. Most of their interactions involve addressing the needs of coordinators rather than those of the public or customers. Ayudantes provide logistical support to coordinators in order for the different segments that constitute a crossing to flow uneventfully.

Bajador Unloader. Often used in vernacular ballads written in reference to drug trafficking, the term *bajador* was initially used in the context of drug transportation, and in reference to unskilled, amateur robbers who would ambush more senior traffickers along smuggling routes. The ballads, known as *narcocorridos*, portray bajadores not only as low in the hierarchy of drug trafficking, but as ignorant of the unwritten rules of the drug trade, particularly those concerning professionalism, respect and trust. In human smuggling, the term bajador is often used in reference to thieves that may ambush groups of border crossers in transit (De Leon, 2013; O'Leary, 2009). In the context of this book, bajador groups are small cohorts of primarily male members, who, aware of smuggling routes and drop house locations, forcefully remove migrants from their original smuggling facilitators. These actions have often been labeled in Maricopa County as full-fledged kidnappings. Bajadores are known for their reliance on violence and weapons, and for the conduction of ransom negotiations with the families of those they hold captive. In this sample the most extreme cases of smuggling-related violence (for example, sexual assault against men and women; torture; assault and even murder) often involved bajador-initiated activity.

Bajón The practice of stealing a load of border crossers from a smuggling facilitator by a bajador; the loss of a group of migrants to bajadores.

Bordo, el   The Edge. Euphemism for the Border; a quasi-uninhabitable, inhospitable region.

Bracero   Worker recruited through the Bracero Program. A guest-worker scheme developed between the Mexican and the US government, Bracero ensured the supply of cheap labor to address employee shortages that prevailed in the United States during World War II (Andreas, 2013). It is estimated that from its inception in 1942 until 1964 when it was phased out, five million braceros were contracted by growers, ranchers and the US railroad industry (Kalavita, 2010).

Caminador   Walker. Those who guide groups of border crossers through sections of the desert and/or the smuggling trail. Caminadores usually work in pairs, assisted by more junior "walkers" in training.

Cangrejo   Crab. Used as a nickname.

Chacho   Nickname of young male.

Chato   Nickname for Flat-nosed.

Comadre   Singular term used in reference to close female kin or kith who is informally expected, in the absence of the mother, to perform all the social roles associated with raising a child; a woman with whom a close, kin-like relationship of support and trust is established and maintained.

Coyote   Smuggler. One of the most common terms used in reference to those engaged in the facilitation of irregular border crossings. The term draws from Mesoamerican indigenous tradition where the coyote (*Canis latrans*) is often characterized as a trickster, a "scorned outsider and the culture-hero" (Ellis, 1993) capable of evading its captors. Coyotes provide one of the few transit alternatives available to those unable to secure the protection of visas or passports to target geographical destinations.

Enganchador   Hooker, recruiter. Enganchadores often scout potential clients among friends and relatives and offer them plans and financial strategies to migrate extra-legally. They are also known to conduct business among men and women arriving to the border without a smuggler, and offer them the services of a specific group of facilitators.

Güera   Blond female.

Ilegal   Undocumented migrant. An adjective rather than a noun, the use of the word *ilegal* has as of late been condemned on a large scale given its racialized and often discriminatory connotations.

Indocumentado   Undocumented migrant.

Linea, la   The border—most commonly, the patrolled sections along the border.

Migra (la)   US Immigration service.

Narco   Drug trafficking organizations.

Norte, El   The North—euphemism for United States

Mojarra, mojarrita   Undocumented migrant, derived from the term *mojado* (wet).

Otro Lado, El   The Other Side. Euphemism for the United States.

Pasando gente   Passing people. The act of smuggling irregular border crossers.

Perrera   Dog catcher; kennel. US Border Patrol vehicles often used to transport those detained while attempted to cross the border extralegally. Perreras have often been at the center of controversy over the mistreatment of border crossers in detention, given their excessive heat or cold, their size and their overcrowding (Nuñez and Heyman, 2007; Slack and Whiteford, 2011).

Pollero   Chicken handler. Human smuggler.

Pollo   Chicken. Irregular migrant; irregular border crosser.

Primera   First class. Top-of-the-line smuggling services involving high cost, decreased risks and faster border crossings and transits.

Rayo   Thunder. Used as a nickname.

Valentía   Courage.

References

Aguiar, J. C. 2010, "Stretching the border: smuggling practices and the control of illegality in South America," *Global Consortium on Security Transformation (GCST) New Voices Series* 6.

Agustín, L. 2006, "The disappearing of a migration category: migrants who sell sex," *Journal of Ethnic and Migration Studies*, *32*(1), 29–47.

Agustín, L. M. 2007, *Sex at the margins: migration, labour markets and the rescue industry*, Zed Books.

Ahmad, A. N. 2011, *Masculinity, sexuality, and illegal migration: human smuggling from Pakistan to Europe*, Ashgate Publishing.

Al-Hajj, A. 2008, "Smugglers force African refugees off boat; 39 dead," *USA Today*, September 10, 2008, http://usatoday30.usatoday.com/news/world/2008-09-10-1859913522_x.htm (accessed 15 December 2013).

Andreas, P. 2001, *Border games: policing the US Mexico divide*, Cornell University Press.

Andreas, P. 2013, *Smuggler Nation: How Illicit Trade Made America*. Oxford University Press, New York.

Andreas, P. and Greenhill, K. M. 2010, *Sex, drugs, and body counts: the politics of numbers in global crime and conflict*, Cornell University Press.

Andreas, P. and Wallman, J. 2009, "Illicit markets and violence: what is the relationship?" *Crime, Law and Social Change*, *52*(3), 225–229.

Antonopoulos, G. A. and Winterdyk, J. 2006, "The smuggling of migrants in Greece: an examination of its social organization," *European Journal of Criminology*, *3*(4), 439–461.

Benton-Cohen, K. 2004, "Docile children and dangerous revolutionaries: the racial hierarchy of manliness and the Bisbee deportation of 1917," *Frontiers: A Journal of Women's Studies*, *24*, 30–50.

Benton-Cohen, K. and Cadava, G. 2010, *Back to the border: a historical comparison of US border politics*, Immigration Policy Center, September, http://oppenheimer.mcgill.ca/IMG/pdf/Back_to_the_Border_090210.pdf (accessed January 20, 2012).

Bilger, V., Hofmann, M. and Jandl, M. 2006, "Human smuggling as a transnational service industry: evidence from Austria," *International Migration*, *44*(4), 59–93.

Billeaud, J. 2006, "Migrant smuggling trial begins in Arizona," *Associated Press*, July 10, 2006, www.apnewsarchive.com/2006/Migrant-Smuggling-Trial-Begins-in-Ariz-/id-ff87763f5aecb1729c097083ebd81c6f (accessed February 16, 2014).

Bolin, B., Grineski, S. and Collins, T. 2005, "The geography of despair: environmental racism and the making of South Phoenix, Arizona, USA," *Human Ecology Review*, *12*(2), 156–168.

Bosworth, M. and Kaufman, E. 2011, "Foreigners in a carceral age: immigration and imprisonment in the United States," *Stanford Law & Policy Review*, *22*, 429.

Bourdieu, P. and Wacquant, L. 1992, *An invitation to reflexive sociology*, University of Chicago Press.

Bourgois, P. 2003, *In search of respect: selling crack in el barrio*, Cambridge University Press.

Bowe, J. 2007, *Nobodies: modern American slave labor and the dark side of the new global economy*, Random House.

Bui, L. and Hermann, W. 2011, "Phoenix police chief reassigned pending review of kidnapping numbers," *Arizona Republic*, March 3, 2011, www.azcentral.com/news/article s/2011/03/03/20110303phoenix-police-chief-city-manager-conference.html.

Burke, G. A. 2006, *Maricopa County Sheriff's Office Incident Report, DR06–34885*, Maricopa County, Arizona.

Cadava, G. 2010, "Arizona has a long history of demonizing Mexican migrants," *Arizona Daily Star*, May, 12, 2010, http://hnn.us/node/126614 (accessed February 15, 2014).

Campbell, J. 2011, "The road to SB1070: how Arizona became ground zero for the immigrants' rights movement and the continuing struggle for Latino civil rights in America," *Harvard Latino Law Review*, 14.

Carlton, A. 2010, "SC touts crack down on hiring, Arizona law yields few results," *News 21*, http://asu.news21.com/2010/08/hiring-of-illegal-immigrants/ (accessed 25 October 2013).

Carr, M. 2013, "We want to welcome the living, not the dead," *State Watch Journal*, *23* (3/4),7–8,www.borderline-europe.de/sites/default/files/background/statewatch-journal-vol23n34.pdf#page=7.

Castro, G. L. 1998, *Coyotes and alien smuggling—migration between Mexico and the United States: binational study*, Mexico City, Mexican Ministry of Foreign Affairs, 3, 965–974.

Chacon, J. M. 2012, "Overcriminalizing immigration," *Journal of Criminal Law & Criminology*, *102*, 613–652.

Chavez, L. 2013, *The Latino threat: constructing immigrants, citizens, and the nation*, Stanford University Press.

Chin, K.-L. 1999, *Smuggled Chinese: clandestine immigration to the United States*, Temple University Press.

Cohn, M. 2012, "Racial profiling legalized in Arizona," *Columbia Journal of Race and Law*, *1*(2), 168–186.

Constable, P. 2014, "White House to send specialists to help recover abducted Nigerian schoolgirls," *The Washington Post*, May 6, 2014, www.washingtonpost.com/local/ protesters-plan-morning-rally-to-demand-nigerian-authorities-take-action-to-rescue-girls/2014/05/06/c3408bba-d514-11e3-8a78-8fe50322a72c_story.html

Cornelius, W. A. 1989, "Impacts of the 1986 US immigration law on emigration from rural Mexican sending communities," *Population and Development Review*, *15*, 689–705.

Cornelius, W. A. 2001, "Death at the border: efficacy and unintended consequences of US immigration control policy," *Population and Development Review*, *27*(4), 661–685.

Cornelius, W. A. 2005, "Controlling 'unwanted' immigration: lessons from the United States, 1993–2004," *Journal of Ethnic and Migration Studies*, *31*(4), 775–794.

Cornelius, W. A. and Lewis, J. M. 2006, *Impacts of border enforcement on Mexican migration: the view from sending communities*, Lynne Rienner Publishers.

Davies, C. 1996, "Nationalism: discourse and practice," in N. Charles and F. Hughes-Freeland (eds), *Practising feminism: identity, difference, power*, Psychology Press, 156–179.

De Genova, N. 2005, *Working the boundaries: race, space, and "illegality" in Mexican Chicago*, Duke University Press.

De Leon, J. 2013, "The efficacy and impact of the Alien Transfer Exit Programme: Migrant Perspectives from Nogales, Sonora, Mexico." *International Migration*, *51*(2), 10–23.

Dimaggio, P. 1979, "Review essay: on Pierre Bourdieu," *American Journal of Sociology*, *84*(6), 1460–1474.

Eagly, I. 2011, "Local immigration prosecution: a study of Arizona before SB 1070," *UCLA Law Review*, *58*, 11–21.

Ellis, L. 1993, "Trickster: Shaman for the Liminal." *Studies in American Indian Literatures*, *5*(4), 55–68.

Emirbayer, M. and Mische, A. 1998, "What is agency?" *American Journal of Sociology*, *4*, 962–1023.

Ermolaeva, E. and Ross, J. 2010, *Unintended consequences of human actions*, University Press of America.

Ferguson, J. 2006, *Global shadows: essays on Africa in a neoliberal world order*, Duke University Press.

Francis, D. 2008, "Mexican drug cartels move into human smuggling," *San Francisco Gate*, March 31, 2008, www.sfgate.com/news/article/Mexican-drug-cartels-move-into-human-smuggling-3221740.php

Galemba, R. B. 2008, "Informal and illicit entrepreneurs: fighting for a place in the neoliberal economic order," *Anthropology of Work Review*, *29*, 19–25.

Galemba, R. 2012a, "Taking contraband seriously: practicing 'legitimate work' at the Mexico–Guatemala border," *Anthropology of Work Review*, *33*, 3–14.

Galemba, R. B. 2012b, "'Corn is food, not contraband': The right to 'free trade' at the Mexico–Guatemala border," *American Ethnologist*, *39*, 716–734.

Galindo, N. 2014, "Police: human smuggler jailed after raping immigrant twice," Valley Central News, April 1, 2014, www.valleycentral.com/news/story.aspx?id=1026126#.U6xFgF9OWwk.

Gamio, M. 1930, *Mexican immigration to the United States*, Arno Press.

Garcia-Marquez, G. 1982, *The solitude of Latin America*, Nobel lecture, March, Oslo, Norway.

Goldsmith, P. R. and Romero, M. 2008, "'Aliens,' 'Illegals,' and other types of 'Mexicanness': examination of racial profiling in border policing," in A. J. Hattery, D. G. Embrick and E. Smith (eds), *Globalization and America: race, human rights, and inequality*, Rowman & Littlefield, 127–142.

Gomberg-Muñoz, R. 2010, *Labor and legality: an ethnography of a Mexican immigrant network*, Oxford University Press.

Gómez, L. E. 2007, *Manifest destinies: THE making of the Mexican American race*, NYU Press.

Gonzalez-Barrera, A. and Lopez, M. H. 2013, *A demographic portrait of Mexican-origin Hispanics in the United States*, Pew Research Hispanic Center.

Gonzalez-Lopez, G. 2005, *Erotic journeys: Mexican immigrants and their sex lives*, University of California Press.

Gordon, I. and Raja, T. 2012, "164 anti-immigration laws passed since 2010. A MoJo analysis," March/April, *Mother Jones Magazine*, www.motherjones.com/politics/2012/03/anti-immigration-law-database.

Grado, G. 2014, "Prosecutor wants executions for human smugglers," *Arizona Capitol Times*, January 10, 2014.

Hagan, J. M. 2008, *Migration miracle: faith, hope, and meaning on the undocumented journey*, Harvard University Press.

Harman, D. 2006, "Illegal migrants persist despite fences, danger," *USA Today*, March 29, 2006, http://usatoday30.usatoday.com/news/world/2006-03-29-illegal-immigration_x.htm.

Hensley, J. J. 2011, "Three in sheriff's office accused of drug, human smuggling," *Arizona Republic*, May 25, 2011, www.azcentral.com/community/phoenix/articles/2011/05/24/20110524phoenix-area-maricopa-sheriff-search-warrants-abrk.html.

Hermann, W. 2011, "Phoenix crime stats audited by Feds after claim," *Arizona Republic*, January 26, 2011, www.azcentral.com/community/phoenix/articles/2011/01/26/20110126phoenix-crime-stats-federal-audit.html.

Hernandez, K. L. 2010, *Migra! A history of the border patrol*, University of California Press.

Hernandez, R. 2006, *Maricopa County Sheriff's Office, Incident Report 06–34885*, Maricopa County, Arizona.

Herrera, Y. 2010, *Señales que precederán al fin del mundo*, Editorial Periférica.

Heyman, J. M. 2013, "'Illegality' and the US–Mexico border," in C. Menjivar and D. Kanstroom (eds), *Constructing immigrant illegality: critiques, experiences, and responses*, Cambridge University Press, 111–137.

Human Rights Watch 2013, *Turning migrants into criminals: the harmful impact of US border prosecutions*, New York.

Ifduygu, A. and Toktas, S. 2002, "How do smuggling and trafficking operate via irregular border crossings in the Middle East? Evidence from fieldwork in Turkey," *International Migration*, *40*, 25–54.

Insley, J. 2004, "Redefining Sodom: a latter-day vision of Tijuana," *Mexican Studies/ Estudios Mexicanos*, *20*, 99–122.

International Organization for Migration (IOM) 2011, "The International Organization for Migration and people smuggling," Immigration and Border Management Programme's Fact Sheet, www.iom.int/jahia/webdav/shared/shared/mainsite/activities/ibm/10-IOM-IBM-FACT-SHEET-People-smuggling.pdf.

International Organization for Migration (IOM) 2013, *World Migration Report 2013*, Genève, CH.

Isacson, A., Meyer, M. and Davis, A. 2013, "Border security and migration: a report from Arizona," Washington Office on Latin America, Washington DC.

Izcara-Palacios, S. P. 2012a, "Coyotaje y grupos delictivos en Tamaulipas," *Latin American Research Review*, *47*, 41–61.

Izcara-Palacios, S. P. 2012b, "Opinión de los polleros tamaulipecos sobre la política migratoria estadounidense," *Migraciones Internacionales*, *6*, 173–204.

Johnson, A. 2009, "In Mexico's drug wars, fears of a US front," *NBC News*, March 9, 2009, www.nbcnews.com/id/29516551/ns/world_news-americas/t/mexicos-drug-wars-fears-us-front/.

Jones, A. 2008, "A silent but mighty river: The costs of women's economic migration," *Signs*, *33*(4), 761–769.

Kalavita, K. 2010, *Inside the State: The Bracero Program, Immigration and the INS*. Quid pro Quo Books, Louisiana.

Khosravi, S. 2010, *The "illegal" traveller: an auto-ethnography of borders*, McGraw-Hill.

Kiefer, M. 2006, "Coyote Law still untested by the jury," *Arizona Republic*, August *18*, 2006.

Koestler, F. 2010, "Operation Wetback," *Handbook of Texas Online, Texas State Historical Association*, www.tshaonline.org/handbook/online/articles/pqo01 (accessed May 25, 2014).

Koser, K. 2008, "Why migrant smuggling pays," *International Migration*, *46*, 3–26.

Koser, K. 2009, "Why migration matters," *Current History*, *108*(717), 147–153.

Krissman, F. 2005, "Sin coyote ni patron: why the 'migrant network' fails to explain international migration," *International Migration Review*, *39*(1), 4–44.

Kunambura, A. 2014, "Zim border posts conduits for human trafficking," *Newsday*, May 10, 2014, www.newsday.co.zw/2014/05/10/zim-border-posts-conduits-human-trafficking/.

Kyle, D., and Dale, J. 2001 "Smuggling the state back in: agents of human smuggling reconsidered." Kyle, D. and Koslowski, R., eds. *Global human smuggling: Comparative perspectives*. Baltimore: Johns Hopkins University Press.

Kyle, D. and Koslowski, R., eds. 2001 *Global human smuggling: Comparative perspectives*. Baltimore: Johns Hopkins University Press.

Kyle, D. and Scarcelli, M. 2009, "Migrant smuggling and the violence question: evolving illicit migration markets for Cuban and Haitian refugees," *Crime, Law and Social Change, 52*(3), 297–311.

La Jeunesse, W. 2006, "Arizona sheriff uses anti-smuggling law to target illegal immigrants," *Fox News*, May 11, 2006, www.foxnews.com/story/2006/05/11/arizona-sheriff-uses-anti-smuggling-law-to-target-illegal-immigrants.

Landolt, P. and Da, W. W. 2005, "The spatially ruptured practices of migrant families: a comparison of immigrants from El Salvador and the People's Republic of China," *Current Sociology, 53*(4), 625–653.

Lara-Valencia, F. and Fisher, J. 2013, "Immigrant informal labor in times of anti-immigrant rage: insights from Greater Phoenix," in L. Magaña and E. Lee (eds), *Latino politics and Arizona's immigration law SB 1070, immigrants and minorities, politics and policy*, Springer Science+Business Media, 129–144.

Leighninger, L. 2003, "Arizona's treatment of its Hispanic residents during the Great Depression," *Journal of Progressive Human Services, 14*, 85–91.

Los Angeles Times. 2010, "A hostile Arizona," April 16, 2010, http://articles.latimes.com/2010/apr/16/opinion/la-ed-arizona16-2010apr16

Lukinbeal, C., Arreola, D. and Lucio, D. 2010, "Mexican urban *colonias* in the Salt River Valley of Arizona," *The Geographical Review, 100*(1), 12–24.

Magana, R. 2008, *Bodies on the line: life, death and authority on the Arizona-Mexico border*, unpublished dissertation, University of Chicago.

Maricopa County v. Alfaro-Martinez, 2008, *Phoenix Police Departmental Report 2008-81762874*. Maricopa County Superior Court CR2008-164618.

Maricopa County v. Armenta-Campoy 2009, *North Mesa Justice Precinct Release Questionnaire*. Maricopa County Superior Court, CR2009-123885-001DT.

Maricopa County v. Armenta-Campoy 2009, *Presentence report data sheet*, Maricopa County Superior Court, CR2009–123885–001DT.

Maricopa County v. Arriaga-Ortiz 2009. *Plea Agreement.* Maricopa County Superior Court, CR2009-109756-001DT.

Maricopa County v. Arriaga-Ortiz 2009. *Presentence report*. Maricopa County Superior Court, CR2009-109756-001DT.

Maricopa County v. Becerra Robles 2009. *Phoenix Police Department Report.* DR200991074559. Maricopa County Superior Court CR2009-144399-014DT.

Maricopa County v. Chacon-Perez 2009, *Phoenix Police Department Report.* DR2009–91254216, pp. 3–5, Maricopa County Superior Court CR2009–153051–002DT.

Maricopa County v. Cruz-Rosette 2009, *Presentence report*, Maricopa County Superior Court CR2009–174973–001DT.

Maricopa County v. De Jesus 2009. *Phoenix Police Department Report.* DR2009-91074559. Maricopa County Superior Court CR 2009-144399 012DT.

Maricopa County v. Diaz- Cisneros 2007. *Maricopa County Sheriff's Office. Supplemental Report* DR#:07172363. Maricopa County Superior Court CR2007-008582-012DT.

Maricopa County v. Garcia-Medina 2007, *Phoenix Hostage Case Investigative Findings*, Maricopa County Superior Court CR2007–174702001DT.

Maricopa County v. Gonzalez-Tagal 2007. *Maricopa County Sheriff's Office Report DR 07-129137.* Maricopa County Superior Court CR2007-143833.

Maricopa County v. Jara Montelano 2009, *Arizona Department of Public Safety Report Number 2009–026212*, Maricopa County Superior Court CR2009–007473–001DT.

Maricopa County v. Lopez-Guiron 2006. *Letter of Support.* Maricopa County Superior Court CR2006-006640-004DT.

Maricopa County v. Martinez-Ponce 2007. *Affidavit.* Maricopa County Superior Court CR2007-008279-18DT.

Maricopa County v. Martinez Ponce 2007, *Motion for aggravated circumstances*, Maricopa County Superior Court CR 2007–008279–18DT.

Maricopa County v. Medina-Meraz 2009, *Phoenix Police Departmental Report 2009–91705299*, Maricopa County Superior Court CR2009–168462–001DT.

Maricopa County v. Nazario-Chavez 2006, *Presentence report*, Maricopa County Superior Court CR2006–172798–001DT.

Maricopa County v. Orozco-Izazaga 2009, *Phoenix Police Departmental Report 2009–91466538*, Maricopa County Superior Court CR2009–159890–002DT.

Maricopa County v. Robaina 2006, *Affidavit list*, Maricopa County Superior Court CR2007–008279–001DT.

Maricopa County v. Saavedra-Trujillo 2009. *Intake sheet.* Maricopa County Superior Court CR2009-006051.

Maricopa County v. Salazar-Hernandez 2006, *Sheriff's Office Incident Report # (DR) 06–034885*, Maricopa County Superior Court CR2006–005932–003DT.

Maricopa County v. Sanchez-Reyes 2009a, *Probable cause statement from Rafael Sanchez-Reyes*, Maricopa County Superior Court CR 2009–168539–004DT.

Maricopa County v. Sanchez-Reyes 2009b, *Presentence report*, Maricopa County Superior Court CR 2009–168539–004DT.

Maricopa County v. Serna 2005, *Arizona Department of Public Safety Offense Report DR2005–045899*, Maricopa County Superior Court CR2009–007798–001DT.

Maricopa County v. Torres-Alvarado 2009. *Presentence report and Intake Sheet.* Maricopa County Superior Court CR2009-166647-001SE.

Maricopa County v. Zuniga 2007, *Presentence report*, Maricopa County Superior Court CR2007–008279–005DT.

Maricopa County Attorney's Office (MCAO) 2005, *Maricopa County Attorney's Office Annual Report*, Phoenix, Arizona.

Marquez, G. 2008, Personal Interview, Phoenix, Arizona.

Martinez, D., Reineke, R., Rubio-Goldsmith, R., Anderson, B., Hess, G. and Parks, B. 2013, *A continued humanitarian crisis at the border: undocumented border crosser deaths recorded by the Pima County Office of the Medical Examiner, 1990–2012*, The Binational Migration Institute, The University of Arizona.

Massey, D. 1993, "Theories of international migration: a review and appraisal," *Population and Development Review, 19*(3), 431–466.

Massey, D., Durand, J. and Malone, N. 2003, *Beyond smoke and mirrors: Mexican immigration in an era of economic integration*, Russell Sage Foundation Publications.

McConnell, E. D. 2013, "Latinos in Arizona: demographic context in the SB1070 era," in L. Magana and E. Lee (eds), *Latino politics and Arizona's immigration law SB1070*, Springer, 1–18.

McLeod, J. 2005. "Feminists re-reading Bourdieu," *Theory and Research in Education, 3*(1), 11–30.

McNay, L. 1999, "Gender, habitus and the field: Pierre Bourdieu and the limits of reflexivity," *Theory, Culture and Society, 16*, 95–117.

McNay, L. 2003, "Agency, anticipation and indeterminacy in feminist theory," *Feminist Theory, 4*(2), 139–148.

Meeks, E. V. 2006, "Protecting the 'white citizen worker': race, labor, and citizenship in South-Central Arizona, 1929–1945," *Journal of the Southwest*, *48*, 91–113.

Miller, J. R. 2011, "Arizona sheriff: wildfires likely started by Mexican drug traffickers, smugglers," *Fox News*, June 22, 2011, www.foxnews.com/us/2011/06/22/arizona-sheriff-wildfires-likely-started-by-mexican-drug-traffickers-smugglers/.

Myers, A. 2010, "Arizona beheading raises fears of drug violence spilling into the US," *CNS News*, October 29, 2011, www.cnsnews.com/news/article/arizona-beheading-raises-fears-drug-viol (accessed on January 30, 2011).

NALEO (2012) "Statement on SB1070 Supreme Court Ruling," 25 June.

Nash, R. 2003, "Pierre Bourdieu: the craft of sociology," in M. Peters, M. Olssen and C. Lankshear (eds), *Futures of critical theory: dreams of difference*, Rowman & Littlefield, 187–196.

Naylor, R. T. 2009, "Violence and illegal economic activity: a deconstruction," *Crime, Law and Social Change*, *52*(3), 231–242.

Nevins, J. 2010, *Operation gatekeeper and beyond: the war on "illegals" and the remaking of the US–Mexico boundary*, Routledge.

Nill-Sanchez, A. 2010, "Russell Pearce: immigration brings 'drug trafficking, human smugglers, child molesters, gang members,'" *Think Progress*, September 7, 2010, http://thinkprogress.org/security/2010/09/07/176255/russell-pearce-crime/.

Nonini, D. 1997, "Shifting identities, positioned imaginaries: transnational traversals and reversals by Malaysian Chinese," in A. Ong and D. Nonini (eds), *Unground empires: the cultural politics of modern Chinese transnationalism*, Routledge, 204–228.

Nordstrom, C. 2007, *Crime, money, and power in the contemporary world*, University of California Press.

Nuñez, G. Heyman, J. 2007, "Entrapment Processes and Immigrant Communities in a Time of Heightened Border Vigilance." *Human Organization*, 6(4), 354–365.

Nuñez-Neto, B. and Vina, S. 2005, "Border security: fences along the US international border," Congressional Report Service, Report RS22026, Washington DC.

Oberle, A. P. and Arreola, D. D. 2008, "Resurgent Mexican Phoenix," *Geographical Review*,*98*, 171–196.

Officer, J. E. 1987, "Yanqui Forty-Niners in Hispanic Arizona: interethnic relations on the Sonoran frontier," *The Journal of Arizona History*, *28*, 101–134.

O'Leary, A. 2009, "The ABC of Migration Costs: assembling, bajadores and coyotes." *Migration letters*, 6(1), 27–35.

O'Leary, A. O. 2008, "Close encounters of the deadly kind: gender, migration, and border (in) security," *Migration Letters*, *15*, 111–122.

O'Leary, A. O. 2009, "Mujeres en el cruce: remapping border security through migrant mobility," *Journal of the Southwest*, *51*, 523–542.

O'Leary, A. O. and Sanchez, A. 2011, "Anti-immigrant Arizona: ripple effects and mixed immigration status households under 'policies of attrition' considered," *Journal of Borderlands Studies*, *26*, 115–133.

Ortega Melendres et al. v. Arpaio 2013, *First Amended Complaint (Class Action)*, United States District Court District of Arizona. CV07–2513-PHX-MHM.

Ortner, S. 2006, "Introduction: updating practice theory," in Sherry B. Ortner (ed.), *Anthropology and social theory: culture, power, and the acting subject*, Duke University Press, 1–18.

Pavlich, K. 2013, "Human smuggling picking up steam in Southern Arizona," *Townhall Magazine*, June 27, 2013, Townhall Magazine, http://townhall.com/tipsheet/katiepavlich/2013/06/27/human-smuggling-picking-up-steam-in-southern-arizona-n1628952.

Pickering, S. 2011, *Women, borders, and violence*, Springer.

Pickering, S. 2014. "Floating carceral spaces: border enforcement and gender on the high seas," *Punishment & Society*, *16*(2), 187–205.

Pickering, S. and McCulloch, J. (eds) 2012, *Borders and crime: pre-crime, mobility and serious harm in an age of globalization*, Palgrave Macmillan.

Provine, D. M. and Sanchez, G. 2011, "Suspecting immigrants: exploring links between racialised anxieties and expanded police powers in Arizona," *Policing and Society*, *21*, 468–479.

Randall, A. 2009, "Mexican drug cartel violence spills over, alarming U.S.," *New York Times*, March 2, 2009, www.nytimes.com/2009/03/23/us/23border.html (accessed on January 30, 2011).

Reuter, P. 2009, "Systemic violence in drug markets," *Crime, Law & Social Change*, *52*(3), 275–284.

Reynolds, S. 2014, *Mexico's Unseen Victims: Field Report*, Refugee International, Washington DC.

Robbins, T. 2008, "The man behind Arizona's toughest immigrant laws," *National Public Radio—Morning Edition*, March 12, 2008, www.npr.org/templates/story/story.php?storyId=88125098.

Robinson, V. and Segrott, J. 2002, *Understanding the decision-making of asylum seekers*, Home Office Research Study 243, Home Office Research, Development and Statistics Directorate, www.irr.org.uk/pdf/understand_asylum_decision.pdf.

Rochkind, D. 2009, *Altar, Sonora: the business of smuggling*, Pulitzer Center on Crisis Reporting.

Romero, M. 2006, "Racial profiling and immigration law enforcement: rounding up of usual suspects in the Latino community," *Critical Sociology*, *32*, 447–473.

Romero, M. and Serag, M. 2005, "Violation of Latino civil rights resulting from INS and local police's use of race, culture and class profiling: the case of the Chandler Roundup in Arizona," *Cleveland State Law Review*, *52*, 75–96.

Rosas, G. A. 2004, *Barrio libre (the free 'hood): transnational policing and the "contamination" of everyday forms of subaltern agency at the neoliberal United States–Mexico border from way, way below*, unpublished doctoral dissertation, University of Texas, Austin.

Rose, A. 2012, "Death in the desert," *The New York Times*, June 22, 2012, www.nytimes.com/2012/06/22/opinion/migrants-dying-on-the-us-mexico-border.html

Rubio-Goldsmith, R., McCormick, M., Martinez, D. and Duarte, I. 2006, *The "funnel effect" and recovered bodies of unauthorized migrants processed by the Pima County Office of the Medical Examiner, 1990–2005*, Binational Migration Institute at the Mexican American Studies and Research Center, University of Arizona.

Salt, J. and Stein, J. 1997, "Migration as a business: the case of trafficking," *Journal of International Migration*, *35*(4), 467–494.

Santos, F. 2012, "Key element of Arizona immigration law survives ruling," *New York Times*, September 6, 2012, www.nytimes.com/2012/09/07/us/key-element-of-arizona-immigration-law-survives-ruling.html?_r=0 (accessed February 16, 2014).

Schick, K. 2010, Personal email communication, April 1.

Sewell, W. 1992, "A theory of structure: duality, agency and transformation," *American Journal of Sociology*, *98*(1), 1–29.

Slack, J. and Whiteford, S. 2011. "Violence and Migration on the Arizona-Sonora border." *Human Organization*, *70*(1), 11–21.

Spener, D. 2004, "Mexican migrant-smuggling: a cross-border cottage industry," *Journal of International Migration and Integration/Revue de l'integration et de la migration internationale*, *5*, 295–320.

Spener, D. 2009, "Some reflections on the language of clandestine migration on the US Mexico Border." Panel on Migration, Religion and Language. International Congress of the Latin American Studies Association, Rio de Janeiro, Brazil.

Spener, D. 2009a, *Clandestine crossings: migrants and coyotes on the Texas–Mexico border*, Cornell University Press.

Spener, D. 2009b, *Some reflections on the language of clandestine migration on the Mexico–US Border*, 28th International Congress of the Latin American Studies Association, Rio de Janeiro.

Spitzer, D., Neufeld, A., Harrison, M., Hughes, K. and Stewart, M. 2003, "Caregiving in transnational context," *Gender and Society*, *17*(2), 267–286.

State Department 2013, *108th US Congress: Intelligence Reform and Terrorism Prevention Act of 2004*, Public Law 108.

State of Arizona 2010, *Senate Bill 1070*, State of Arizona Senate, Forty-ninth legislature, second regular session.

Stellar, T. and Ibarra, N. 2002, "Scoring heating, soaring toll," *Arizona Daily Star*, September *29*, 2002.

Stern, R. 2009, "One thousandth illegal immigrant prosecuted under state's human smuggling law," *Phoenix New Times*, April *24*, 2009.

Tellez, M. 2008, "Community of struggle: gender, violence, and resistance on the U.S./Mexico Border," *Gender and Society*, *22*(5), 545–567.

Teo, S. Y. 2003, "Dreaming inside a walled city: imagination, gender and the roots of immigration," *Asian and Pacific Migration Journal*, *12*(4), 411–438.

Thomas, A. 2009, "Our 1000th successful human smuggler prosecution," *Illegal Immigration Journal—Maricopa County Attorney's Office*, Retrieved from www.illegalimmigrationjournal.com/spotlight/andy.cfm?id=61 (no longer available online).

Tietz, J. 2012, "The US-Mexico border's 250 miles of hell," *Men's Journal*, April, www.mensjournal.com/magazine/the-u-s-mexico-borders-150-miles-of-hell-20130103.

Torres, J. 2004, *Alien smuggling: new tools and intelligence initiatives*, statement of John P. Torres before the House Sub-committee on Immigration, Border Security and Claims, May 18, 2004, Washington DC.

Trevizo, P. 2013, "Ministering in brutal Altar, Mexico," *Arizona Daily Star*, May 19, 2013, http://azstarnet.com/news/local/border/ministering-in-brutal-altar-mexico/article_aacee843-0c7a-5b0a-bbce-3afbfe8c8ba4.html.

Tucson Citizen 2006, "Our opinion: Az conspiracy prosecution of migrants fails," August 30, 2006, http://tucsoncitizen.com/morgue/2006/08/30/24369-our-opinion-az-conspiracy-prosecution-of-migrants-fails/ (accessed February 15, 2014).

United Nations High Commissioner for Refugees 2013, Global Trends 2013, Geneva, Switzerland.

United Nations Office on Drugs and Crime (UNODC) 2011, *The role of organized crime in the smuggling of migrants from West Africa to the European Union,* United Nations, New York.

United Nations Office on Drugs and Crime (UNODC) 2013, *Migrant smuggling*, www.unodc.org/unodc/en/human-trafficking/smuggling-of-migrants.html (accessed May 26, 2014).

US Department of Justice 2012, *Department of Justice files lawsuit in Arizona against Maricopa County, Maricopa County sheriff's office, and sheriff Joseph Arpaio*, press release, May 10, 2012, www.justice.gov/opa/pr/2012/May/12-crt-602.html.

US District Court v. Mirtha Veronica Nava-Martinez 2013, Order. Criminal no. B-13-441-1. Filed in the Southern District of Texas, December 13, 2013.

US Federal Bureau of Investigations (FBI) 2011, *Uniform Crime Report, Crime in the United States. 2011: Property Crime.* FBI: Washington DC.

US Immigration and Customs Enforcement (ICE) 2013, *Enforcement and Removal Operations Fiscal Year 2013*, ICE Immigration Removals. Washington, DC.

Valle, N. R. 2005, "El coyote en la literatura de tradición oral,", *Revista de Literaturas Populares*, *5*, 79–113.

Valle del Sol et al. v. Michael B. Whiting et al. 2010, *Plaintiffs' proposed motion for preliminary injunction and memorandum of points and authorities in support (oral argument requested)*, United States District Court for the State of Arizona, CV-10–01061-PHX-SRB.

Valle del Sol et al. v. Terry Goddard 2007, *Findings of Fact, Conclusions of Law, and Order*, United States District Court for the District of Arizona, CV07–02496-PHX-NVW.

Van Hear, N. 2004, *"I went as far as my money would take me": conflict, forced migration and class*, Centre on Migration, Policy & Society.

Van Liempt, I. 2007, *Navigating borders: inside perspectives on the process of human smuggling into the Netherlands*, Amsterdam University Press.

Van Liempt, I. and Doomernik, J. 2006, "Migrant's agency in the smuggling process: the perspectives of smuggled migrants in the Netherlands," *International Migration*, 44, 165–190.

Vélez-Ibáñez, C. G. 1996, *Border visions: Mexican cultures of the southwest United States*, University of Arizona Press.

Wagner, D. 2006, "Human trafficking profits spur horrors: vicious organizations move thousands of immigrants through valley every day," *The Arizona Republic*, http://archive.azcentral.com/specials/special42/articles/0723drophouse-main2.html.

Watson, F. 1977, "Still on strike! Recollections of a Bisbee deportee," *Journal of Arizona History*, 18(Summer), 171–184.

Weber, L. and Grewcock, M. 2011, "Criminalising people smuggling: preventing or globalizing harm?" in F. Allum and S. Gilmour (eds), *The Routledge handbook of transnational organized crime*, Routledge, 379–390.

Weber, L. and Pickering, S. 2011, *Globalization and borders: death at the global frontier*, Palgrave Macmillan.

Wheaton, E. M., Schauer, E. J. and Galli, T. V. 2010, "Economics of human trafficking," *International Migration*, 48, 114–141.

Whiteford, S., Slack, J., Martinez, D. and Pheiffer, E. 2013, *In the shadow of the wall: family separation, immigration enforcement and security*, The Center for Latin American Studies, University of Arizona.

Williams, P. 2009, "Illicit markets, weak states and violence: Iraq and Mexico," *Crime, Law & Social Change*, 52(3), 323–336.

Zhang, S. 2007, *Smuggling and trafficking in human beings: all roads lead to America*, Greenwood Publishing Group.

Zhang, S. 2008, *Chinese human smuggling organizations: families, social networks, and cultural imperatives*, Stanford University Press.

Zhang, S. 2009, "Beyond the 'Natasha' story—a review and critique of current research on sex trafficking," *Global Crime*, 10(3), 178–195.

Zhang, S. and Chin, K.-L. 2002, "Enter the dragon: inside Chinese human smuggling organizations," *Criminology*, 40, 737–768.

Zhang, S. and Chin, K.-L. 2003, *Characteristics of Chinese human smugglers: a cross-national study*, Final Report, US Department of Justice.

Zhang, S. X., Chin, K.-L. and Miller, J. 2007, "Women's participation in Chinese transnational human smuggling: a gendered market perspective," *Criminology*, 45, 699–733.

Index